It's My Job

Mike Stanton-Rich

It's My Job
by Mike Stanton-Rich

Online editions may also be available for this title. For more information, please visit us at www.lulu.com.

www.Lulu.com

Lulu Enterprises, Inc.

Table of Contents

Introduction

Has anyone ever asked you the question: "What do you do?"

Occasionally I will respond with a sarcastic answer like, "I do lunch," or, "I try and get up in the morning." It may amuse the questioner for a moment, but they truly want an answer on which they can hang the rest of the conversation.

I have discovered that when I tell someone I am pastor, that means they will probably not tell me about their drunken affair from the night before, or how they cheated the government out of their taxes. And that's okay; I really don't need to know that information. They are more likely to talk about why they haven't been to church, or maybe ask a deep question like: "What happens after you die?" This is the normal kind of conversation that comes with my job title.

I have not always been a pastor. I have done a number of things in my life. Each job came with a different set of questions. When I worked in television, someone usually asked, "Have you met…(insert somebody currently starring on TV)?" When I was teaching, they always asked, "What do you teach?" When I was working on the farm, I always got, "You're not going to do that the rest of your life are you?"

Over the years, I have learned that this is a loaded question. In asking what someone does, we are in a sense asking: "Who are you?" Though we have learned that our jobs no more define us than the clothes we wear, or the car we drive; we do know that what we do for a living is an important part of the puzzle of our lives.

I like the question, "Who are you?" Dependent on the time of day, my mood, or what just recently frustrated me, I can answer that question a myriad of ways and never be lying. When I am striking the keyboard and knocking out another paragraph, I am a writer. Yet there are other parts of the day that being a writer is the furthest thing from my being.

The hours I spend at my day job in the local church, I think of myself as pastor, but I am often getting the question, "Are you sure you're a pastor?" Maybe because I refuse to wear a tie, or because I don't present myself like other pastors that people have met.

I know I am a father and husband, a brother and son, but I also think of my family most times as my friends. I am an educated person. I have more degrees than most humans ought to have, but I am not so sure where my diplomas are right now, so I must not be that bright.

One of the best answers that has ever been given to that question, "Who are you?" were the words: "I am who I am." It was such a profound answer that even to this day in the Hebrew Bible when you come across those basic words, the proper name for God, you are supposed to say something else. I am convinced that our answer to the question is so powerful, that whatever we might say, it will be a fraction of all that we are.

This little volume captures just a fraction of all that I have done, and all that I am. I am thankful to be able to recall such a varied working life. I am thankful for the material rewards that have come my way because of the different jobs I have held. I am also thankful that whatever I write about my career now will just be a portion of all that I might write in the future.

May you enjoy these stories of my making a living, and ultimately, my making a life.

Odd Jobs

Most of us have had them. They are the jobs you get before you have a driver's license, and before you learn about deductions and 401(k) distributions. Those were the simpler days, when after a job well done you were handed cash, something you could actually spend-the kind of stuff that didn't come with a stub that narrated your debt to society. I remember when those green bills felt so good in my pocket, and at the same time I couldn't wait to break them and spend them.

I had several odd jobs along the way. Most of them were pretty common, but some of them stand out. I share those now with a disclaimer:

Everything you are about to read is true, though not everyone who shared the experiences remembers the events with the same kind of clarity or truth.

Squirrel Sitting

Like the time my friend paid me to watch his flying squirrel. I think I was supposed to make a dollar a week while he was on vacation, and all I had to do was give the squirrel some food every day. Easy money, I thought. Be careful with easy money, it will often get the best of you.

My friend Andy was one of the best baseball players around at age nine. He played for a baseball team called the "Tankers" (that's the kind of mascot you get when you live on a military base-scatted among the Pirates and the Cubs were teams with names like Tankers, Minutemen, Bombers, and Cadets). He loved his team so much that he named his pet flying squirrel "Tanker."

Now I am not sure about this, but when I grew up there were lots of exotic pets that are probably illegal today. I was told that the turtles I had as a kid cannot be bought in many places today because of state laws and the like. I remember friends having protected species of various kinds in their back yard, but I have never met another that owned a flying squirrel.

When Andy left for vacation that summer, I was given the keys to his house, strict instructions on how to feed it, and plenty of food to keep it happy for two weeks. But Andy never mentioned that this squirrel really loved to try his wings, and took great pains to escape from captivity. Imagine my surprise when I went to feed it, and it bounded through the little door out into the kitchen. This happened on the second day, so I only had 12 more days to endure.

Tanker was a flyer. He would fly from the top of the refrigerator to the kitchen table, from the table to the cabinets, from the cabinet to the doorframe, and back to the floor. But never did I see him fly back into the cage. I knew he had, because the food would be eaten every day, but Tanker preferred to spend his days elsewhere.

Every day I would try to catch him; every day I would fail. When I brought my Dad in to help, the squirrel took one look at his baldhead and decided that this would be his next perch. Flying from the cabinet to the top of his head, Tanker almost made Dad hurt himself. I am not sure what squirrel feet feel like on the top of your head, but from the dancing and screeching that was going on, it must not have felt very good.

Andy was due to return on a Saturday, so on the Friday night before we went to the house to try one last capture. We went armed with a net, and a paper sack, and we crafted a plan to get the squirrel back in the cage. What fun that was.

Tanker was in rare form. He was bouncing from one cabinet to the other, from the refrigerator to the table to the floor, and back again. Dad even caught him in the net one time, but could not hold on long enough to get Tanker in the cage. After an hour of failed attempts in a rather small kitchen, the flying squirrel was still loose.

We decided to leave a note on the door to the kitchen—"Tanker is loose, be careful."

On Saturday morning, I went to feed "Tanker" for the final time. I set the little cup of food in the cage, and looked down, and there was the squirrel, asleep and peacefully calm.

I closed the cage door, took the sign off the kitchen door and went back home to tell the folks. It may have been the hardest I ever worked for $2 dollars in my life.

Snow Shoveling

I have not always lived in the Deep South. Those who are truly from the Deep South can sense it as I walk into the room. There is this sixth sense in the Deep South for knowing your own kind, and there is something that tips people off immediately to this fact.

So when I tell a story that seems quite implausible for a kid from Alabama, you've got to see the whole picture. There are not many folks that hail from Alabama that can claim they made spending money through the winter shoveling snow.

First, when it does snow every blue moon in Alabama, it usually never stays more than a day, so there is no shoveling required. Second, because there is usually warning before a snow, people have already gone to the grocery stores to buy extra milk and bread for at least a week, so nobody gets out on the day of the snow, again, no shoveling required. Third, I don't believe I have ever seen a bonafide snow shovel sold in Alabama, so there must not be much of it going on.

When I made my spending cash shoveling snow, we lived in North Dakota. We only lasted one winter up there. My mother who was born and bred in the Deep South endured one snow season and swore that she would not spend another day in thirty below temperatures for no one, not even a man she loved and lived with for twenty-five years. My Dad took the hint and planned to retire when spring came in May.

But that one winter was excellent for pocket money. Every morning I was out in the dark shoveling our own driveway so that Mom and Dad could get to work (it was dark because we only had about 7 hours of daylight for much of the winter). The temperature would be hovering about twenty degrees below zero and the neighbors would look out and see me shoveling and offer me $5 or $10 dollars so that they could stay in the warm house. I could sometimes make $20 dollars on a real cold morning.

Across the street from us was a young couple in their twenties. He worked away from home three or four days a week and his wife was pregnant. He had to be gone a week in December and he made me a proposition: keep his driveway clean and he would treat me right.

It snowed every day that week, and I was out every morning shoveling the driveway. Even after I had sprained my ankle in the last basketball game before winter break, and was on crutches, my father agreed to do our driveway so that I could do the neighbors' and keep my end of the agreement.

The pregnant wife drove her BMW out of the garage every day, and I struggled to use a shovel and crutches at the same time.

He got back from his trip on the Friday before Christmas. I was anticipating big money after his wife told him how dedicated I was, and how easy I had made it for her. Seven days of shoveling, a generous neighbor with a BMW, I should have been set for a month. I had already planned how to spend that huge sum of money before I even had it.

He dropped off an envelope when we were at the store on Saturday morning. Inside there was a Christmas card, with the simple words scrawled "Thanks from Paul and Ann." Inside the card was a $10 dollar bill.

I wasn't sure what to do so I asked Dad what he thought. He said simply, "I am sure he treated you right. Just some folks notions of right are different than others."

The next time Paul was going out of town, he asked if I could help out again. "I'm sorry. I'll be pretty busy," was my reply.

It snowed the evening he left, and Ann was out trying to move snow around in her advanced state of pregnancy. She was in no shape to be shoveling snow, so I came to the rescue. She handed me a $5 dollar bill and told me not to tell Paul that she had paid me. "He's such a cheap skate, I want him to believe that I shoveled snow all week. He will owe me big time"

Every day I would shovel the driveway, go in the house for hot chocolate with a beautiful pregnant woman, and come away with a $5 dollar bill. Paul never found out.

Sears Delivery

The town where I grew up was small. We were not big enough to have a movie theater, or many fast food restaurants. But we were just the right size, and the right kind of town for a Sears Catalogue Store.

Growing up, everyone knew about the Sears catalogue. It was a long-time fixture in rural society. When it wasn't being used for shopping, it could be found in the outhouse. Even when I came along, when hardly anybody had an outhouse, we kept the Sears catalogue in the bathroom just for reading.

The annual catalogue came out every year in the spring, sometime around Easter. That would be the day that your mail was sure to be several hours late because the mail carriers were busy toting those ten-pound books. We would wear it out those first few days, turn down pages, and start picking out all the things we wanted but would never get. Even in a good Christian home, the Sears catalogue was always the most read book in the house. It may not have been as prominently displayed as the family Bible, but it was certainly read cover to cover more times than the Holy Book.

As a kid, I couldn't wait for the Christmas catalogue to come out, because we only went to the big city about once a year. The Sears Christmas catalogue had all of the newest and best toys listed, and it was more portable, so I could sneak it back to the bedroom and read it before I went to bed. In fact, I learned to read and do business math using the Christmas catalogue. To this day, a book with colored pictures is still more interesting to me.

So, why have a catalogue store? It was completely possible for anyone to order merchandise anywhere in the country and have it delivered right to their door. All you had to do was fill out the forms, enclose the check or money order, and a week or two later the mailman would leave a package on your doorstep. But did you ever have a washer and dryer delivered to your doorstep? It is much more difficult.

First, the mail carrier would not be the one to do it. Second, those other delivery companies were not the kind of folks to leave large items on your porch. Even if the delivery was made, you would still need help installing the appliance and filling out the warranty papers and the like---the catalogue store handled all of those things.

The other great thing about the catalogue store is that you never had to pay for the item until it came so checks were never lost in the mail, and if the order didn't come out right, you had someone in your corner.

In my hometown, my best friend's family owned and operated the catalogue store. They did a terrific business, and they were hard-core Sears folks. Sears furnished their house and completed their wardrobe. If you were not sure about an appliance, or piece of hardware, all you had to do was drop by their house and you could see the item in use. They could give first-hand testimony to the reliability and quality of most products in the catalogue.

Jimmy and I would toss a Sears basketball all day long into a Sears basket and backboard set mounted on a pole with the Sears approved brackets. We would settle into a Sears couch in the den and watch afternoon programs on a Sears model television. When we got thirsty we would go to the Sears refrigerator and pour a cold drink into a Sears glass set. As we got older, Sears was there for pocket money.

This may have been one of the most interesting part-time jobs I ever had. The catalogue store was a family owned business and operation, so Jimmy was expected to pitch in on a regular basis so that he could continue to have a place to sleep and food on his plate. There were busy times of the year where I would get paid to help out in the family business. My favorite time was the week before Christmas.

Nearly every day that week a big truck would roll into town, and would unload the hundreds of packages destined for the honored places beneath Christmas trees all over town. Often the truck would come after school, so I would check in with the store on my way home. It was a great way to pick up $5 dollars for an hour or two of work.

The high paying job at the Sears catalogue store was weekend delivery and installation. Most of the appliances were delivered during the week and installed by a professional. Those who couldn't be home during the week, had to settle for a less than professional delivery and installation. Jimmy and I would get the washer and dryer in the back of his pick up, drive out to the house, and then spend an hour or two installing them (of course the professional could do it in 30-45 minutes). Depending on the job, I could make $20 dollars for an afternoon's work (not bad for the 1970's).

I learned more on deliveries about my hometown than most anything I did. I will never forget installing a washer and dryer on a back porch that had almost no wood on it. We actually set the machines on floor joists and hooked up the plumbing and electricity while looking down at a dozen dogs and cats sleeping on the ground. I was actually scared to make a wrong step because if I missed the two by six stud I would have stepped on some kind of an animal.

On another delivery we brought a deep freezer to a house that already had one. We were supposed to deliver the new one and take the old one back to the store. She said that nobody told her that she was supposed to empty the freezer and defrost it before we came. We spent an hour removing food from the freezer and putting it in ice chests. When we finally got the new one in and the old one on the truck, the woman looked and said, "I didn't order this model."

We made a call back to the store, and you could hear Mr. Bond turning beet red over the line. Cursing under his breath he told us to put everything back as it was and he would deal with the woman himself. Seems she made a mistake, and she did order that model, it just looked smaller than she imagined. The regular guy went out and installed on Monday, and she had the old one defrosted and cleaned out.

On several occasions we delivered large screen TV sets (this was in a day when 27 inches was considered large) to homes that needed doors and windows more than they needed an entertainment center. We arrived at one home that had no glass in the windows, and the only door had a hole about large enough for a size ten shoe. In the den was a homemade cabinet with two padlocks on it. The owner said, "You can't be too careful with a new TV."

By far, the most memorable delivery was when we brought a riding mower to the home of an 80-year-old man with a fairly small yard. He told us that he had used a push mower for the last 60 years, and he was just getting too old to push the mower around. After spending several hundred dollars on a riding mower, he realized that he did not have a clue how to operate it. Part of our job was to acquaint him with the mower and make sure he knew how to do the basics. Nobody told us that the man had never driven a car in his life, so we had bitten off more than we could chew.

Starting the engine was no problem, it was just like the push mower, but explaining the brakes and clutch and gears was nearly impossible. Jimmy and I both drove it around his yard showing how various things worked, we nearly cut the entire lot while we were there it was so small, and then it was his turn to drive.

We had left a couple of swipes of grass to practice with before he jumped into the seat. He mashed in the clutch, put it in gear just as we told him, then we watched in amazement as he let out the clutch and proceeded to tumble off the back of the mower. The mower raced forward cutting everything in sight, including flowers and newly planted shrubs before crashing into a pine tree.

I made sure that the old man was okay while Jimmy turned off the mower. He got up and dusted himself off and then offered my buddy a deal. "How about cutting my grass every week? I've got this brand new mower that does the job great, when I'm not driving it."

An Entrepreneur at Fifteen

Most kids have big dreams, like being an astronaut, or a fireman, or the President. And if they don't have big dreams, they all want to make lots of money.

At age fourteen, I wanted to be a farmer when I grew up. I discovered early that my dream would not lead to a fortune and also discovered that this was a pretty big and daunting task for a kid who didn't come from a farming family. The likelihood of a person being able to buy the land and equipment from scratch is about the same as a person without a high school diploma getting into Harvard. It may happen, but not very often.

All through high school I entertained that dream of being a farmer by being a member of the Future Farmer's of America. Not just a member, a leader. From the tenth grade through graduation I served in various roles, from Reporter to President. I even won a local award for being the most promising agricultural student in the area. I was on all kinds of teams that went to county and state tournaments including the land judging, livestock judging and dairy judging teams (It must be noted that these teams were not as prestigious as being on the school football team). I even entered the regional public speaking contest one year but came in second to a guy who spoke for fifteen minutes about grass (he had excellent hand gestures my advisor said). By the time I finished high school, I had completed all of the requirements to obtain the highest award given in the State of Alabama, the State Farmer Degree. When I think about it, that was not bad for a kid who never had the chance of farming in the future because all my family had was about an acre of land just outside of the city limits, and it was covered in trees.

The single biggest factor in obtaining the State Farmer degree was to have an FFA project that netted at least $500 dollars (this was in 1978, so that was a stretch for most projects). Some of my friend's projects were: raising steers for sale, growing ten acres of peanuts or corn, and hatching and raising domestic quail and pheasants. My project was one of the firsts of its kind in my high school; I ran a greenhouse and grew vegetable plants for wholesale and retail markets.

This all came about because I had pestered my father for over a year to help me with a project. Raising cattle was out, because we didn't have the land. Raising a crop was out, because even if I had rented land, I had no equipment. My father suggested that I could raise dogs, since we already had five or six in the yard, but we decided that there was no market for poor behaving mixed breed "sooners." (After my Dad's constant expression--"The sooner they leave the better.")

In the fall of my sophomore year, Dad gave me a $500 dollar loan and said that if I could figure how not to lose it, I could have my project. So I did some serious research. One of the self-study projects that I had done in fourth period Vocational Agriculture class was on "ornamental horticulture" or the growing of plants for beautifying the home. The book came complete with diagrams on how to build a greenhouse, how to start seeds, how to mix soil for transplants, and then how to market plants for sale. I read every word of the book, and believed firmly that I could make a go of it. Then I prepared my budget. The greenhouses they suggested would cost upwards of $2000 dollars, and the related materials another $1000 dollars. My loan wouldn't cover it.

The day that I made the budget, I had to meet my mother downtown, so I walked by the feed and seed store on the way to her office. It was early fall, and there were all kinds of fall plants like cabbage, broccoli and short season tomatoes for sale. I looked at what they had, which were all in terrible shape, and I looked at the price tag, and I had this brainstorm, "I can do better than that."

I talked to the manager and asked him if he would be interested in carrying some locally grown plants in the store, knowing that he was getting plants trucked in from over two hours away. He said, "I can't break my contract with the plant farm, but I am not making any money with them. If you can provide me with better plants, I will let you compete with them."

It was September and I began hatching my plan for the next spring. First, I had to get a couple other stores to back me, then I had to build a greenhouse, then I needed to figure out how to raise seedlings, then I had to find the guts to follow through on the plan.

Through the fall my Dad and I worked on clearing a few trees and making a place for a small greenhouse in the backyard. This was not easy considering there were lots of trees--tall, 40 year old pine trees. Though neither of us was injured, and none of the structures on the property was destroyed, after cutting the fourth tree, we decided that we had done enough, and brought in a pulpwood company to clean up the logs in the yard.

I spent about a week leveling ground with a shovel and rake, and then spent a weekend building a misshapen greenhouse. It was not pretty, but when the sun was shining, it was 25-30 degrees warmer than the outside temperature. By the end of December, I had spent about $250 dollars and had a working greenhouse.

By January, I had to start growing the seedlings for transplant so that plants would be available the first week that the frost warning was gone. This was usually around March 1st, so I had about eight weeks to pull it all together.

Seedlings are easy to grow and care for. They don't take up much space, you can keep them warm with a heating pad like device, and they don't take much water. I planted four varieties of tomato seeds, and a few other vegetables, and looked to the day that I could transplant.

Seedlings germinate in seven to ten days, and are ready for transplant in about fourteen. You can plant a thousand seeds in a few minutes, but it takes hours upon hours to set transplants in individual pots. Around day fourteen I was cursing the day I had ever dreamed of building a greenhouse. That was the most tedious and backbreaking day of the whole project. My schedule planned for three weeks of plants to sell, so once the transplants started, I was busy.

Of course, I was still in high school, so all of the chores had to happen before and after classes. I would have to water plants twice a day, make sure the vents were open for heat to escape, and then turn on the heaters at night. It was a pretty intensive couple of months getting the plants ready for sale. This schedule was made more complex by the weather, the baseball coach, and even by the dogs that hung out in the yard.

Though winters are not terrible in Alabama, there were a few nights that temperature went down below freezing, and the little artificial heat I had at night was not enough to keep the plants warm. I devised some auxiliary heat by keeping trashcans full of water in the greenhouse during the day that would warm up to about eighty-five degrees before dark. They kept the greenhouse a little warmer. I also made shelf coverings out of newspaper that seemed to hold the heat of the plants better. Many nights I would wake up at 2 a.m. to check the temperature in the greenhouse, and also to make sure that the circuit breakers hadn't blown. I could not wait for frost season to be over.

During the days, we had the opposite problem. The sun would come out, and it would get too warm. My mother or father would be home for lunch every day, and would try to check the temperature and the vents, but most days the plants had to wait until after 3 p.m.

That's when the baseball coach got in the way. I had anticipated playing varsity baseball that year. The coach had seen me play thought that I had talent, but wanted to check my devotion to the team. Practice would start at 3:15 p.m., and we would usually finish by 5:00 p.m., leaving me about an hour of daylight to get my chores done. This was usually not a problem, until one day a small tornado ripped through town while we were in class. The winds were very high for about an hour, there was rain, hail, and lots of lightning, but when classes let out at three o'clock, everything was calm. I took the bus home that day to check on my greenhouse and skipped practice.

I figured the coach would understand my needing to check my investment out (lucky thing, because the plastic was ripped off the frame, and was wrapped around a tree), the plants had been wind blown but not destroyed. I spent the afternoon getting things back in place. The next morning I went by to explain the situation to coach and the only thing he would say to me was: "Two miles." (Meaning I owed him two miles of running before I would be allowed to practice with the team again.) My high school baseball career ended with that tornado. I figured that I had too much invested in my project to run two miles for a humorless coach to play on a team that had a long history of losing. So I spent the afternoons back at the house.

And if the weather or the coach didn't complicate matters, the dogs did. As I had mentioned earlier, we had a bunch of dogs that hung around the house. They were all strays or pups of strays, so we didn't really own them. But we fed them and let them lay around the yard.

When the greenhouse went up, they found it interesting. They thought it was a big doghouse, and before the covering was even put on it; they would lie on the floor anticipating having a roof over their head.

On a cold day, if the door were left open, they would sneak in and lay in the heat (imagine the smell of a greenhouse full of dirty dogs heated up to ninety degrees!). I would always get them out before I closed the door, and I took great pains to discourage them from chewing on things in the greenhouse (they especially liked treated wood), but occasionally I would miss one.

Like the time I came home from school and discovered a big hole in the side where a dog scratched through. I am guessing that I was sleepy that morning and didn't see the dog settle down for a nap while I was watering. On another occasion, when I had propped the door open before leaving for school, I must not have secured the block enough, and I am betting that the dog that went in for a nap was more than ready to escape when the temperature rose to over ninety degrees after the door slammed shut. He didn't bother leaving through the door that was easier to fix, but chose a more direct route through the side.

Finally after a long eight weeks waiting for spring, I got to sell my first plants. Dad and I loaded up a little station wagon (that is a story in itself) and hit all of the seed stores in the community that had promised to buy or take plants on consignment. We put out the sign in front of the house, and folks began stopping. Fifty cents a-piece or three for a dollar was what I made at home, twenty-five cents each from the store. It is amazing how quarters and half dollars add up over a few weeks.

I found one of the best tactics for selling plants was to show up at corner grocery in the country when all of the old guys were playing checkers. Guerrilla marketing I called it. I could bring a flat of plants in, lay them on the counter buy a cold drink, and before long these guys would lay down their checker gambling earnings on plants that they probably didn't need. One of them told me, "We're just so pleased to see a high school kid doing something constructive with his time, we can't help but support you."

"Buy the last flat in my car so I can go home then," I replied.

He handed me a ten-dollar bill, "Will that do it?"

It was 10:30 a.m. on a Saturday morning and I was out of plants, you bet.

By the end of March, I had nearly $1500 dollars in my bank account. I wrote a check for $500 dollars to Dad to repay the loan, and I thought I was rich. We moved that summer, and the greenhouse had to come down. I never even rebuilt it at the new place because I couldn't bear the thought of another winter tending to those time consuming plants. So I sat on my earnings, and I believe they were still in the bank until I went to graduate school. If I looked on my bookshelf closely today, I might still find a book or two that was bought with greenhouse money.

Mixon Farms

The job that probably did more to influence my life than most was the year I spent working for Mixon Farms. There were both positive and negative influences that are probably responsible for why I am doing what I do now. More than that, the way I do things now were deeply influenced by those experiences. Those days on the farm never seem as far away as the twenty-five plus years it has been. But I have never been so far away from my roots as I am right now.

Why was that year so indelible? Let's start at the beginning.

Do you remember what you first wanted to be when you grew up? Like most folks, there was a long list of things that I wanted to be. But when I was in the ninth grade, I had no dream that was clearer than wanting to own land and farm it.

This is a difficult proposition if you were not raised on a farm or you did not inherit one. There are not many people who could make that decision in high school, get a diploma, buy the acreage and start farming. Even those who were rightly poised to do so, the sons and daughters of farmers, they headed off to college more often than not to earn a degree that would take them away from the farm. I even had this selfish dream of maybe being adopted by a farmer whose child had snubbed them for the city life, and I would inherit a family farm to call my own.

Like I said, it's not that easy. So I spent my high school years preparing to do what I wanted to do. I was a loyal member of the Future Farmers of America. I took vocational agriculture each day as an elective along with all of my college prep courses, and I took every available opportunity to learn the ins and outs of farming from uncles and neighbors.

I even chose to attend summer school for two summers to take my required courses so that I would have the afternoons free my senior year. I planned to work on a farm every afternoon for credit, and for a little bit of money.

I discovered that school year that it was perfectly legal to make less than minimum wage if you were a co-op student in high school. In fact, my boss was not required to pay any more than two-thirds of minimum wage (I remember getting a total of $1.67 per hour that year).

That was truly just a little bit of money in 1978. A 20-hour week with taxes deducted came to just about $30 dollars per pay check. There was not a farm in the county that could not afford working someone to death for $30 bucks a week. Mixon Farms happened to make that deal with me.

To understand Mixon Farms, one has to start with the boss. Her name was Violetti Bailey. She had been married to a Mixon before he died, and she received the farm as his widow. All of her children were off doing other things, so she decided to run the farm herself. She was the only lady farmer in that part of the world, so she had to keep a tough exterior, and a tough demeanor. She spoke her mind and ran a tight ship. I am sure she could do all the work herself, but she hired a couple of men and me to look after the place.

The other guys were the farm manager named Mack, who everyone else in the community called "Boogerman" and his sidekick, Tommy James. The two looked after almost 200 acres of crops, 200 acres of pasture with about 150 head of cows, and a hog lot that constantly had about 100 pigs being fattened for market. There were all kinds of tractors and trucks to keep working, and a bunch of chores that would never get done. We spent most of everyday catching up on things that were supposed to be done the week before. Don't let anyone fool you by saying that farming is a low-stress job. I have never seen a "To Do" list as long as it was at Mixon Farms.

I worked all day most of the summer before school started, and then went to half days when my senior year began. It was a long school year.

I got out to the farm about 1:00 p.m. every day, and was usually greeted with a list of chores that had to be done by 5:00 p.m. Many days I had to work with someone, and I preferred that it be Tommy James. He would gently correct my mistakes and was very quiet and patient. "Boogerman" was not that way. He was always hypercritical, and fumed as he personally corrected my mistakes, and then complainer about having to pay me anything at all, "You're getting school credit for this, and I pay taxes, I don't see why we owe you a cent for being out here." I was thankful after a few months there that they trusted me with a number of chores I could handle on my own, so I would often spend full afternoons without either of them. I probably enjoyed that the most.

So what did I learn on the farm?

First of all, *I learned the meaning of hard work.*

I had friends that spent their afternoons working for other local businesses, but few of them every worked up a sweat, and even fewer were required to lift anything over 100 pounds at any time (there was some kind of law about that I am told).

August on the farm meant both heat and heavy lifting as we cut, baled and stacked hay for the winter. One week before school started we stored over 3,000 bales of hay for the upcoming winter. The person stacking in the eaves of the barn usually had his hat pressed to the tin roof heated by a long summer day. We took a thermometer up there one day and it displayed 115 degrees. When I finally got home at the end of the day, I was spent. I could drink gallons of water before bed and never get up in the middle of the night.

During harvest season that year we had over 150 acres of peanuts. I would work from 1 p.m. to 9 p.m. five days a week, and then on Saturdays from 6 a.m. to 6 p.m. I am pretty sure this was against the law, but the money sure seemed good. (Mrs. Bailey actually upped my pay during harvest season because she was paying lots of other part-time help better than minimum wage---one week I made about $200 dollars after school. That was big money in a day when I could buy a car for $400-500 dollars. It was a real let down when winter came and the weather was bad and I could only work 15 hours at $1.67.) To this day I can still put in a hard day of physical labor, I just don't recover as quickly as I did at seventeen.

Not only did I learn the meaning of hard work, *I learned that sometimes hard work doesn't pay all that well.* Beyond my small paychecks, I observed the arbitrariness of farm prices and products and how profit and loss could happen in the blink of an eye. We spent lots of time in a field, brought a couple of trailers of new peanuts to the warehouse, only to get mediocre prices that barely made expenses. That same afternoon a productive cow died, and all the profit for the day was shot. Some years, Mrs. Bailey would get a new car after harvest season, and Mack would get a new truck, but there were many other seasons when they wondered how all of the bills at the feed and seed store would get paid. This lesson by itself taught me that maybe my dream of farming was not going to happen.

In spite of that lesson, *I learned that working hard and working the land provides plenty of life-long entertainment.* There are not many folks with advanced degrees in the humanities that can say they have castrated pigs and calves, or had their arm in the womb of a heifer. I have amazed friends and colleagues for years with stories of cold mornings waiting for a cow to give birth so that I could pull a breech calf out by its hindquarters. People are still amused by my little car that grew corn in the floorboard that grew pretty thick because of the daily addition of hog manure flakes from my boots. Once a Japanese ambassador peppered me with questions for hours about how we grew peanuts in fields of 40 acres or more. I can actually say that a federal marshal arrested me one afternoon in the spring as we prepared for planting season. As I burned off the last year's crop I was chased down and nearly handcuffed by a guy who was just doing his job and protecting the community from unlawful arsonists. Mack made sure that fire permits were filed in the future.

I will never forget when Mrs. Bailey showed us all up one winter when she single-handedly caught a calf in a pen that her hired help had tried to do for a week. She even did it in her sparkly, gold heels after a trip to the beauty parlor. I would still pay good money to see that on videotape. I would pay for a CD of the priceless cursing of the "Boogerman" after she told him to go move that calf back to the new pasture.

More than anything, *I learned from the farm that in the midst of constant change, there is some constancy.* Every season there seemed to be new methods, and new equipment to learn. Every crop rotation brought a new set of lessons from a plot of land, and yet every season, there was something constant. I am still moved by sunsets, clear, cold mornings, and the smell of fresh rain, all because I was so close to them and they were so constant for that year of my life.

When I went off to college, Mrs. Bailey took me aside and thanked me personally for my work that year. She knew that I would enjoy college, and told me that if I were smart, I would take that education as far as it would take me because only fools and old women like her would put up with the farming life. Then last, she apologized for all the hassle that the "Boogerman" had given me over the year, but she added, "He didn't mean it personally, he is like that with everyone."

The First Church Job

Near the end of my senior year of high school, I announced to family, friends and my church that I was thinking about becoming a preacher. I was seventeen years old, and lifetime commitments didn't come easy, so I said, "I was thinking," rather than "I will become." But no one understood the subtleties that I intended.

This decision came when I was on a mission trip to Costa Rica. Unlike any other mission trip I have ever been on, this one involved very little work, but required lots of riding on a bus. We road a yellow school bus all over that country. One day we road over twelve hours in 100 degree heat, that was actually quite an adventure for folks from rural Alabama.

You get lots of time to talk when you are on a bus that long. I had already scoped out the only two teenage girls that were on the bus, and after a couple of days discovered that they really didn't want anything to do with me, so the last part of the trip I talked to everybody else.

There were Methodist preachers complete with white shoes and ties, little old ladies who had never been out of the country, and this middle-aged mayor from a small town in East Alabama who thought it would be interesting to see how his church's mission dollars were being spent. He was a little different than your average Methodist layperson, a little crusty, a little more outspoken, and even a bit irreverent at times. It was his irreverence that was most appealing to me.

We became fast buddies, and talked for hours on end. He told me about playing college football at a junior college that didn't require him to go to class. I told him about my work on the farm, and how I wanted to farm for a living but would probably end up as a veterinarian or an agriculture teacher. Wayne looked me in the eye, and said, "I know it's none of my business, but you don't look like someone that would enjoy working with animals all day. Have you ever thought about working with people?"

I could truthfully say that I hadn't. I had thought about being an agricultural missionary of some kind, but the thought of working with people did not interest me in the least. I enjoyed people, just never thought about working with them.

That question came early on that 12-hour bus ride up and down some volcano in the sticks of Costa Rica. I had to ponder that question all-day and then through the night as we slept on the pews of a ramshackle church in the middle of what I would call nowhere. The gas produced from a dinner of rice and beans kept me up even longer with that question seared in my skull: "Have you ever thought about working with people?"

We got back on the bus early the next morning, and Wayne and I proceeded to talk some more. I asked him, "What kind of people work were you talking about yesterday?"

"Have you ever thought about being a preacher? Lord knows we've got a bunch of bad ones out there. Some don't even know how to dress themselves," he whispered under his breath as he glanced over at one of the preachers on the trip wearing a plaid shirt, a striped tie, and his trademark white shoes.

"You've got to be kidding," were the first words out of my mouth. I discovered he wasn't.

"You are just the kind of guy that I would want my children to look up to. I think you could do the church a lot of good." And then we didn't talk for a couple of hours, so I stewed on that new information in the heat and humidity of that yellow school bus.

The last day of this mission tour, Wayne introduced me to his pastor that was on the trip. "We've been talking it over, how would you like to work at our church this summer?"

"What?" was about all I could stutter. I had not made any big plans, but my Dad had something worked out with a construction company if I wanted it. I was going to make about $200 dollars a week to put toward school. Then came their offer.

"We figure we can pay you about $50 dollars a week, give you room and board, a little gas money and a great experience. Will you think about it?" queried

Wayne.

"I'll think about it. But I won't promise you anything."

So I came home from Costa Rica and announced: "I am thinking about becoming a preacher."

It scared my folks; after all they had supported me through four years of an obsession with farming, even though they knew I would never do it. They had whole-heartedly supported me going off to State College because it was cheap. But they were not so sure what to think about this new announcement.

I told them about the job offer, and they laughed. "What church in their right mind would hire a kid straight out of high school?" And that pretty much clinched the deal. I was going to show them that there was a church just crazy enough to hire me and house me for a summer.

So I counted down the days to graduation and my first job in a church. I told the church that I was "only thinking about becoming a preacher" and to not have high expectations for me. Wayne assured me that the church had almost no expectations for $50 dollars a week. "Come spend time with our kids, do what the pastor asks you to do, and get to know the community and you will do fine."

So a week after graduation I packed up my car and headed for the little town of Cedar just over an hour from my home. It was the first time I had lived away from home and I was kind of looking forward to it. This was not your typical summer job, and I felt so special. When I arrived that Saturday morning, I discovered just how untypical it was.

The family they had me living with was a little on the eccentric side. They were not originally from that town, and they were not small town people. So they rubbed most of their neighbors and most of the church folks the wrong way. But they were gracious to host me and thought it would be a fun summer for all of us.

There was really nothing planned on that first day, since the next day was Sunday, I would see everybody at church. So I had a little freedom. I settled in and unpacked, which took me all of fifteen minutes, had a light lunch with the

McMillan's, and asked them if it was okay for me to ride around town in the afternoon. "No problem…we won't be back for supper but help yourself to anything in the fridge." My first day and I am left almost totally to myself. This was going to be a great job

After driving around for an hour, which allowed me time to cover every street and highway in Cedar, I began making plans for Saturday night. In my hometown, everybody hung out at the Dairy Queen parking lot, so anybody new to town could wander down there and get into as much mischief as they wanted to on a Saturday evening. I figured there must be some place similar in Cedar. I was wrong.

What I did discover were a bunch of cars parked behind the high school at the tennis courts, and I knew how to play tennis, so that was where I went. This was a pretty brash thing to do for someone who was not really sure about working with people for a living, and who, for most of my life, had been an introvert. But this was a new job and a new me, and I'll be darned if I was going to pass up the opportunity of meeting up with other teens in the community.

I was able to worm my way into a little friendly one-set match with a guy with similar ability. As we played I got drilled with questions about who I was, where I was from, what I was doing, and the like. When we finished the match and I had lost 7-5, we went to the side where several others were sitting and the big question came: "Where are you living?"

"I am staying with the McMillan's on Clover Street."

"The dog burners?"

"The what?"

"The dog burners, the guys who torched the bulldog last week."

"Torched a bulldog, you're kidding?"

"Nope. Seems the folks across the street had this bulldog named 'Flash' and he was caught humping the McMillan's poodle, so they set him on fire."
"No?"
"Yeah, it was big news. The ASPCA is taking them to court. It should be a wild summer at their house."

So I went home to an empty house wondering if the neighbors would come torch me while the McMillan's were away. When they got home, and I am still wondering how I had the courage to be so confrontational at seventeen, I asked them to explain the story to me.

They were apologetic that I had to find out that way, but felt like I shouldn't be burdened on my first day with their problems. They explained that Flash broke through a window screen, scratched through a door, and had snapped at both of them as they were trying to pry the dogs apart. Rex said that he had read that gasoline annoyed a dog's skin and would make them head for dirt, so he thought he would try it. "I only used a cup, and most of that hit the floor in the kitchen. I didn't think it would harm him."

"And I had read that dogs will run from flames, so I started flicking matches at him as he was headed toward the window," said Millie, the petite wife. "I never expected him to catch on fire."

"All the flames were out before Flash crossed the street to his house. It really wasn't as bad as everybody made it out to be. The ASPCA is not even going to take up the case…there goes Flash now," Rex pointed to a very ugly bulldog chasing a car down the street.

"And we still have puppies on the way," added Millie.

The start to a fun summer.

Part of my job was to spend time with Senior Citizens each week. There was a Senior Center downtown that offered a hot meal and a couple of hours of fellowship Monday through Friday. They set it up so that I could eat lunch at the center a couple of days a week.

The first day I went they introduced me to the Domino ladies. There were four of them that played serious, cutthroat dominos, usually for money. So every day before or after lunch there was a guaranteed game in town. The center director didn't especially like them gambling, but she knew that they weren't losing lots of money and she just avoided confronting them. "They are old enough to be my grandmother," she said, "and my grandmother would tan my hide if I corrected her about something like this."

So a couple days a week I would show up at the Senior Center, and the domino ladies would fawn over me. After about two weeks, they would invite me into the game when somebody was missing for a doctor's appointment or family visit. After a month, they asked me to gamble with them.

I suggested that it might not be proper for a church worker to play for money. "No problem!" they chimed together, "We'll play for donuts."

A box of Krispy Kreme's cost about a dollar, so the losing team would have to pay about fifty cents each. That sounded fair, and not much like gambling. Those ladies knew a sucker when they saw one.

Blind Emma was the oldest of the bunch, and she had all of her faculties but sight. She knew what was happening in the world and was not afraid to share her opinion on anything. She was also the best player at the table. She memorized all of the moves and knew exactly what was laid down on the table at any time. She knew what was in her hand by feel, and she could just about tell what was in everybody else's hand by what they played.

Her constant partner was Miss Ruby, and it looked like she had eaten more than her share of the donut winnings. She knew exactly what to play so that Emma would score on nearly every turn. Even though my math skills were decent, I still had to think about every move and count in my head each   multiple of five. Ruby did it unconsciously as she hummed show tunes under her breath.

When I played, it was usually with Miss Jewell, because her partner Miss Annie was always going to the doctor and missed lunch frequently. Miss Jewell played pretty well, but was constantly shaking her head when I did something stupid. It would get her rattled and she would make a poor play that Emma would pounce on. Before we knew it, Emma and Ruby would be scoring 20 or 25 points on every move and we would have nothing to stop them.

After getting beat a few times by Ruby and Emma, I began to wonder how they did it so consistently. They must have had a system. There must have been a mathematical formula. Something kept them winning and I was going to find out what it was.

I began analyzing each game, and nothing seemed out of the ordinary but one thing. The show tunes. When I hum show tunes, I usually stick with one for hours on end. Ruby seemed to have a new one each time it was her turn. Sometime she would hum the same one several times in a game. There were new ones that I knew and old ones I didn't know, and that usually correlated with what she was playing or going to play. Emma supposedly had enhanced hearing because of her blindness, and she could tell the subtle differences in the tunes.

I had caught some elderly widows cheating at dominoes, but did not have the heart to tell them. In total my partners and I lost about eight boxes of donuts through the summer, and I only remember winning once when Emma was at the doctor.

Be careful next time you play dominoes with elderly women is what I say.

Most of that summer job was working with children and youth. That little church in Cedar had about fifteen children and fifteen youth most Sundays. The crowd would double for something special and the kids brought their friends. If food was involved, we might have more than that.

If you can imagine a seventeen-year-old in charge of twenty or thirty youth, you will have an accurate picture of how things went that summer. The crowd was usually wild, loud, and not into following directions. No matter what game we played or activity we tried, there was someone who would get hurt, or their feelings would get hurt, or the property around them would be hurt. All I can say is that parental neglect kept our summer youth program running.

One of the group's favorite games was "Hide and Seek" or a variation of it, "Sardines." They loved for it to get dark outside, and then they would turn off the lights in the building and amuse themselves for hours on end. I remember one game where twenty of us were jammed into a broom closet while the last person looked for us. Then we discovered that all of the cake that someone brought was mysteriously gone after we tumbled out of the closet in laughter.

The most memorable game was what we called the Hide and Seek Grand Championships. The winners would get their name placed in a frame that we would hang in the fellowship hall for perpetuity. There was the single and the doubles championships. Playing with a partner was something unique to that town, and I have never seen it again anywhere.

During the doubles competition we saw some fascinating strategies. Often there were boy-girl teams, and this gave young lovers an opportunity to smooch a bit before getting caught. I never had to police it much because it was a small building and most everybody knew what was going on. One of the best teams was a high school senior named Tim paired with Ricky, his cousin in the seventh grade. Ricky could hide in the smallest places, and Tim was great on defense.

But the most interesting of teams was Randy and Evan. Randy was the oldest member of the group. He was actually a junior college student that lived at home and had nothing better to do than hang out at the church with young kids. He was from one of the poorest families in town but was trying to improve his lot in life. Evan came from the other side of the spectrum. He lived in a modern mansion on the outskirts of town, and was going to graduate the next year and attend West Point. They were an awesome team destined for infamy.

When we began the doubles competition, it was about 7:00 p.m. The ground rules were laid. We all agreed which places in the church were off limits: the sanctuary, the pastor' study, the kitchen, and the furnace room. There was a time limit declared of thirty minutes, and I had the power to declare a winner in case of a tie. It seemed to be a cinch. In fifteen minutes or so there would be a winning team to write on the certificate.

Twelve pairs were playing, and the Bedsole sisters were "it." They knew that the championship was theirs if they could tag the rest of the teams out.

Within ten minutes all but two of the teams had been found and tagged. Only Randy and Evan and Tim and Ricky were left. After another ten minutes, the Bedsole sisters were still looking for them. They figured that the time limit might expire before the teams were found.

I was walking through the sanctuary just to see if they had been hiding out in an illegal place when I heard this strange noise coming from up above. "No way," I thought to myself. Then I heard this crash that sounded like a car coming through the side of a house, followed by the chime of the church bell.

I went to the church entrance, and there were Randy and Evan covered with broken sheet rock, insulation and the attic dust of a century on top of them. Though they were in some pain, you couldn't tell it because they were laughing so hard. They had spent the entire game walking the attic and had planned to climb down out of the bell tower to safety when Randy slipped and dragged the other through the ceiling. Evan said he held on to the bell rope to break his fall.

Just about that time Randy's aunt came through the door yelling about someone ringing the church when the Bedsole sisters tagged the boys and yelled, "You're out!" From the look on Mrs. Smith's face, she was saying the exact same thing to me: "You're out!"

We all went to the fellowship hall to regroup and there were Ricky and Tim, posing on home base, the winners. It was a bittersweet win; because it was the last time we played that summer.

We closed the night in prayer, thanking God that neither of the boys were dead, and hoping that Mrs. Smith would not have a stroke before getting home. I prayed that I would not be fired on the spot. We made plans for a special educational program the next day in which Randy and Evan would teach us the finer points of repairing a ceiling. The certificate was never hung on the wall.

The Road Crew

The job that I had for the shortest time may have been one of the most educational I will ever have. I worked on a road crew for two weeks between a summer job and my first semester of college. I learned enough in those two weeks to know that I never wanted to do that kind of work again, and learned to appreciate those who do it day after day.

Technically, I worked for an independent contractor, Chancellor Construction, but for all intents and purposes, I was employed by the Alabama Highway Department since they paid the bills. We were resurfacing and restoring a four-mile section of highway just outside of the Elba town limits. The "we" was a crew of seven that changed so frequently that there were only two days during the two weeks that an identical crew worked. I learned that seniority was not hard to obtain in that business if you just came to work every day.

As long as the weather was good, we worked ten-hour days, and could expect ten hours of over-time each week. I wouldn't call the weather good, since it was close to 100 degrees each day with high humidity, but it didn't rain, so we worked hard and I made good money, at least compared to other jobs I could have had. It was 1978 and I was making $5 dollars per hour and $7.50 dollars for over time hours. I figured that each day I worked for the road crew was equal to a week's salary with my first church job, which I did the first ten weeks of the summer.

The job began at 6:00 a.m. every morning, and we were gone by 4:30 p.m. with thirty minutes for lunch. Because it was a road crew after all, and it was the middle of August, we paced ourselves. This was not exhausting work. The first day I cleared ditches of debris and held a flag for the pavers. The second day was similar, but by the third day part of the crew quit and the other part was fired, leaving me as the most senior member of the non-skilled labor. There were three guys who handled large machinery who were always there, but they never had to do the jobs I was given.

By Thursday of my first week, I was driving a dump truck and transporting gravel and fill dirt. I am pretty sure that this was illegal, since I was only seventeen and had no training in driving heavy machinery, but that didn't seem to matter to Chancellor Construction. I was a warm body that showed up every morning at 6:00 a.m.

At the beginning of my second week, I was in charge of getting the backhoes back to home base at the end of the day, and by the end of the week I was the boss's personal assistant which meant I drove him to Montgomery on Thursday and Friday. Mr. Chancellor told me I had a future in the construction business if I wanted one. I am guessing that if he hired more high school graduates and made the work a little more challenging, he would find all kinds of people who had a future.

I learned a few things that have proved invaluable over the years, and I share them with you now:

Showing up to work everyday is an admirable trait. I don't know why it comes easy to me, but it does. Whenever I have a job that keeps regular hours, I try to show up at the appointed hours each day. I discovered that this was rare among road crew folks (and other groups too!). Of the seven on the crew, three showed up every morning at 6:00 a.m., a father and son team that ran backhoes and me. The rest came in within the next hour, or didn't come in at all. Jack Danley, one of the more reliable workers who drove heavy machinery, rarely came in at 6:00 a.m. because, by his own admission, "… I had too much to drink, too much at stake with a woman, or too much of an upper right hook after work…I would rather be docked an hour's pay than be decked by my old lady for waking her up at 5:30 a.m."

Follow orders unless they cause injury to yourself or someone else. Jack Danley tried to teach me the ins and outs of the job each day after he showed up. He suggested that if I was directing traffic with the safety flag, and someone deliberately drove past me when they were supposed to stop, I had the legal right to throw rocks at their car. "For their personal safety," he rationalized. He also suggested that I drive the dump truck beyond the speed limit because it saved the company time, and the cops never stop employees of the state. Both of his suggestions seemed a little reckless, but I did give them a second thought. Mr. Chancellor had other ideas: "Why would you listen to a guy who gets beat up every night because he's drinking or fooling around? Use the sense God gave you, boy."

Work hard and you might get promoted. In just two weeks on the job, I had gone from a simple ditch worker to the boss's personal assistant. I contribute this to working hard. Unlike James and Jimmy, the father and son combo who napped on their backhoes every chance they got, and Jack who never came in on-time and often left early, I was a model of hard work, if you could call dump truck driving hard work. James and Jimmy were envious of me, and were quite upset when I was called on to drive the boss to Montgomery on Thursday of my second week. Mr. Chancellor, referring to their sleeping habits, told them that he "didn't want his driver to fall asleep at the wheel, and he was not sure that anybody else on the crew was capable." That remark probably led to my doing the same thing the next day, because James and Jimmy were known to take offense and do horrible things to those that wronged them. One worker's car was mysteriously scratched up the entire passenger side after one altercation. Another worker found himself accidentally covered with about 500 pounds of topsoil after making one of the two mad. The boss knew it would be my last day on the job, so he wanted no incidences, and had me drive to Montgomery on my last Friday to pick up the week's paychecks.

Remember the economy of words. In writing there is such a thing as the economy of language. Many editors look for lots to be said in a few words. I am convinced that the road crew was a good place to learn about this economy. With just a few choice expletives, Mr. Chancellor could get twice as much work out of us. Jack Danley could explain how something worked or how a task was done with a few grunts and hand gestures. The Reedy's, the father and son team could go all morning and all afternoon without ever speaking a word to the crew or each other. Occasionally at lunch they would swap pleasantries, but at work they were almost silent.

This was different from most of the crew that quit or got fired. One day Mr. Chancellor got so annoyed with an employee before lunchtime, he fired him for talking too much and paying no attention to his job. Things were never quieter, and we did everything to avoid Mr. Chancellor the rest of the day.

Hard work can be satisfying. Much of what I do these days is sit in front of a computer, go to meetings and talk a lot. The only time I perspire at work is when the air conditioner is broken, or on a hot day in August when I have to walk to the car to go to a meeting. Otherwise, the clothes I leave home in look much the same when I return.

When I worked on the road crew, the clothes were always drenched in sweat and had a distinct odor at the end of the day, a mix of human sweat, dust, and oil. Though I was tired at the end of the day, I could look back and say, "Hey,

we paved 200 yards today, laid fifty feet of pipe, and got the backhoe fixed."
We weren't going to change the world, but we were making a small corner of it
smoother. There's something to be said for that

I Get Paid for Doing This

My first summer out of college was a winner. I was hired by a little church in the "big" town of Autaugaville, Alabama, population 200. It was no more than a dot on the map, and anyone who had ever been there is still wondering how it founds its way to a map. However, it was a fascinating job, and it kept me from working road construction all summer.

Being the summer youth and children's director kept me busy. The church averaged about 75 people on Sundays, and almost half of the congregation was under 20 years old. The youth group would have as many as fifteen on a Sunday night, and there were enough young kids to field a couple of baseball teams. I know this because we did.

Every Sunday evening there was a youth group activity, and most Sunday afternoons we would do something special with the children. Every Wednesday morning was "Mother's Morning Out" and we would have 25 kids at the church for games, crafts and stories. Every Wednesday evening was "Youth Night" and there would be 25 youth from all over town hanging out at the church.

Baseball or softball rounded out the rest of my schedule. Tuesdays and Thursdays were my semi-pro nights. I played for the Autaugaville Rams, which was a part of the old Negro Association of Alabama. I was told that a number of the stars of the former Negro Baseball League played on the sandlots of the association back in the 1930's. I was one of a few players that crossed the color line because my boss, the church's pastor, was a former college catcher. I was the youth director because the Rams needed a utility player that was good with the glove and could make consistent contact with the ball.

It was semi-professional ball. That meant that there was ticket money collected at every game but none of the players ever saw a dime. Usually the coach would buy beer with the gate receipts, and the boss and I would go home to avoid the brawls that often took place after the team began drinking.

Every Monday the women's softball team would play and I would either be coaching, umpiring or keeping score. Nearly every Saturday was my softball day, and the pastor and I would play on a tournament team that traveled around central Alabama to class B tournaments.

Friday was sometimes my day-off, unless the youth planned an event, and on that day I would find time to play golf, tennis or pick-up basketball. To say the least, it was a very healthy summer. Much of the excitement of that summer happened away from the church, either on the ball field or where I lived.

I lived that summer with a well to do family that employed two maids and a handyman. If I wanted a little excitement, I could go home and watch the sparks fly between the maids and the woman of the house. For ten weeks, there was a hot lunch everyday at noon that was available if I wanted it. The menu never changed. There was a meat (most often it was liver, sometimes country fried steak, occasionally chicken), squash, beans or peas, rolls and iced tea. After about two weeks of liver, I asked if there was something else I could have, and they showed me a freezer full of steaks that I could have anytime I wanted. I rarely missed lunch at the house that summer.

The kids at that house were characters. The oldest child was a year older than me and a student at Auburn University. The youngest was 15 years old, and had more business in jail than in high school. Both were pampered and their mother tried to keep them on a close leash. They were so amazed at my mother turning an 18-year-old loose for an entire summer to live with strangers. They could never figure that out.

Rayford, who was the 15-year-old, had a Porsche that he was only allowed to drive with an adult present. Also, he was never allowed to drive after dark. So I got my share of Porsche driving that summer. I have never driven another since but it was a rush at eighteen. Rayford did a few odd jobs and watched television the whole summer. Nearly ever Sunday and Wednesday night he found a way to make everyone in the youth group angry, so consequently he made me angry. After he was put on restriction for blowing up a tool shed, life with the youth group became simpler.

The oldest, Beth, was in summer school, but she spent nearly every weekend home. She was also supposed to call home every evening and report to her mother. I would guess that my folks checked on me about every two weeks (not much different from now), and after discovering that I still had a pulse and checked on my finances, they would pretty much leave me alone.

I lived in a guest suite of the house and never got the chance to make my bed because as soon as I went to the shower a maid would come by and make it for me. If clothes were on the floor, whether they were dirty or not, a maid would pick them up, wash and iron them, and place them on my bed every afternoon. I learned that summer that this kind of existence was not for me. I actually enjoy having clothes hanging on door handles and socks on the floor. They make me feel at home.

As a gesture to the family for being so good to me, I would always participate as a lifeguard on their community swim day. They opened their pool to the kids of the community one day per week so that the kids could be supervised and learn to swim. Seems the Autuaga River had drowned more than its share of the town's kids through the years so the family saw it as a needed service. Many weeks there would be 50 kids learning to swim and crawling all over each other in the pool.

On Tuesday and Thursday nights I learned what it felt like to be a minority. Usually when the Rams played there were only two of us in the whole stadium that were white. One game I was hit by two different pitches and then walked during a third at-bat because the pitcher kept throwing inside and high. I scored each time I got on base, and that just made the other team mad, so I had to be on guard for high spikes every time someone slid into third base. My boss played catcher, and after his second season in the league, they quit throwing at him, figuring he was not scared in the least.

On one road game near Prattville, we played in what was literally a pasture the rest of the week. We cleared the field of cow pies before infield warm-ups. My teammates wagered the home team that "our white boys" would get six hits between them if the pitcher threw strikes to us. I got the best pitches I had gotten all season, and both of us had three hit games while our teammates made over $200 dollars. (I did say it was semi-professional ball.)

On another occasion we were playing near Montgomery and that pitcher was bound and determined to hit me in the head. The coach flashed me the hit and run sign to advance the runner on first. I knew I was supposed to swing at the next pitch, but I was more concerned with keeping my teeth. The pitch was aimed right at my chin, and as I ducked I swung and laced a double down the left field line. It was one of my best hits all summer and I had my eyes closed.

I keep wondering, as I get older if I will ever have another summer job like it. Most days, whether on the baseball field or at the church with kids, I would always ask myself: "I get paid for doing this?"

A Man of the Cloth

I declared my major early in college. I was studying in one of those really practical, liberal arts departments: Religion and Philosophy. A large number of those majors were working their way through school working in churches or church based organizations. I was no different.

I worked every summer, and all but one semester of my college days in a church setting (I may have actually had the best time as a student that semester, since I could actually be a full-time student, and had a social life—but that semester is a whole other story).

During the second half of my sophomore year and the first half of my junior year, I was working as a youth director at a church in Montgomery, Alabama. It was a large church without a huge number of youth and children. We had some great things going at the church, and I was ready to finish out my schooling on their staff. It would have been a very easy situation to continue, just a few minutes by car from campus, about 20 minutes by bike. I had a great boss, and a great staff to work with. Why would I want to move?

Then I got this call the week of fall finals. It was the District Superintendent from the area where I grew up, and he had a proposition. He knew that I had been through local pastor's school and that I once considered being a student pastor. He also knew that I was familiar with the area. "I would like for you to consider being the pastor of the Dozier Charge."

My throat went dry and my heart sunk. This was the week of finals; I had two exams and a paper to get out of the way before I could think seriously about becoming a student pastor. I had to talk to my boss in Montgomery. I even told the D.S. that while I was at it, I'd better talk to God. He suggested that would be a smart thing to do. So I told him I would get back with him as soon as finals were over.

"No hurry, we aren't going to fill the church anytime soon."

So I did all the talking to everyone I needed to contact, and then called the superintendent toward the end of the week. It occurred to me that maybe I'd better find out why a church was open a couple of weeks before Christmas. There had to be a story behind it. He didn't get very specific on the phone, but indicated that the guy who left in the middle of December had some difficulties, but that he shouldn't be too difficult to follow. This was encouraging, but I still had some issues to work out at my current job. We arranged a meeting for a couple of days before Christmas, and it was my plan to begin in Dozier the last Sunday in January. The D.S. was ecstatic. It should have given me a hint of all that was to come (does the term "sucker" come to mind), but I just thought he was a generally happy person.

I talked to various folks at the Dozier churches by phone, talked to the superintendent, and put a close to my work in Montgomery. January was a very long month. I spent that time collecting all the information I could on the charge, and discovered enough to give me cold feet.

First of all, a "charge" is a collection of churches served by one pastor. This was how the earliest Methodists covered the frontier with churches in the 18th and 19th centuries. Some of the early circuit riders had seventeen churches or meetings that they would cover by horseback. The Dozier Charge in 1981 had four churches that I covered with a Toyota. There was something ancient and yet modern about the whole arrangement.

The four churches were very distinct, and ranged from twelve to 50 in worship. The two smaller churches only met twice a month at 9:30 a.m. (so they alternated Sundays, and gave me fifth Sundays off). The other two churches met every Sunday, but alternated between morning and evening. They too gave me fifth Sundays off because they didn't want to fuss about who could meet in the morning. This kind of schedule was not user friendly, and though I could get it right every Sunday since I was paid to do that, it didn't mean that sometimes people were caught off guard by the calendar.

Dozier, Alabama is in the "Heart of the Wiregrass" which is another way of saying it was in farm country, in the deep southern, central part of the state. It had one flashing yellow light, a bank, a grocery store, a dry goods store and a county school that had about 160 students in grades 1-12. Dozier was the only true town on the charge, the rest of the churches were in little communities that had no shopping, and no road signs to speak of. Searight was a few miles west on the main highway, Cameron's Chapel was several miles north on a less than secondary road, and Oakey Streak was exactly 18.7 miles from downtown Dozier, and was basically in the middle of nowhere. Some folks claimed that you drove first to nowhere, and then kept going to get to Oakey Streak.

After a month of research and anxiety, I was scheduled to meet folks at the churches for the first time on the Saturday before my first sermon. I doubt that I have ever been so nervous before or since. They told me to meet them at the parsonage in downtown Dozier. They said I couldn't miss it because it was the house next to the church with all of the cars out front. They were right.

I entered the house and began to meet my pastor-parish relations committee. That is the group in Methodist churches saddled with the responsibility of overseeing the work of the pastor. Little did they know what they were getting themselves into.

The first question came with a puzzled grimace "How old are you?"

"I just turned 20 in November."

"My youngest grandson is 20," was his reply.

"Have you had that beard long?" asked one of the women

"Over a year."

"I suggest you keep it, it makes you look a little older," she smiled.

"Do you think you can go to school, and serve these churches?" was another question.

"I have been serving churches and going to school since I started. I believe it is possible."

"You realize that we are not a youth group, right?"

After looking around the room, and there being no one under 50, I could nod with agreement.

"Then tell us about what you want to do here."

"It's very simple, I want to be as good a pastor as I can be in the little bit of time I have with you, and I promise to give you the best sermons I know how to give every Sunday."

"Son, if you preach from the Bible every week, it will be pure improvement over what we have had," from one of the younger looking guys on the committee.

After that comment, someone launched into. "This is what you need to know about us…We haven't had a preacher for over two months, the last one left town in the middle of the night in December and took all of the good furniture from the parsonage and left over $1500 dollars in bills at a couple of stores in town. Forgive us if we don't think too highly of preachers right now."

Somebody else chimed in, "He wasn't what you would call a bad man, just a strange one. You'll hear all kinds of stories about him. Most of them will be true. Your best bet is to just go about your business paying it no never-mind."

"We know you're a student, so you won't be here as much as we would like; but believe us, we have been pretty much taking care of things on our own for the past two years. If you will do the preaching, bury our dead, marry our children, and act like you care, you will go a long way here."

Then the meeting basically ended. The superintendent, sent them all home, and then took me out on the roads to see all of the churches. We were gone for about two hours, and he dropped me off at the house, where I would spend the night before preaching my first sermon.

Oakey Streak was scheduled for the first service the next day. I had to leave about 8:45 a.m. to guarantee that I would get there. I got to the church a little early, walked around a bit, and discovered there was no bathroom and no outhouse. There was no one there at 9:10 a.m., but I still didn't want anyone to catch me peeing behind a tree as my first act as pastor. So I made a commitment to hold my water for the next hour and a half. The first question someone asked me when he or she arrived was, "Do you need a drink of water?" I declined.

There were about eighteen people that showed up that first Sunday. They all had the same last name except for two. I discovered they were all related, either by blood or by marriage. And I discovered that if the humidity were high, the piano wouldn't play. I was thankful it was a cool winter morning with low humidity, and we sang several hymns out of the Cokesbury hymnal before it was time to preach. I lost that sermon long ago, and it is probably a good thing, but I remember that first sermon being memorable. People seemed to listen, and the couple of youth that were there were not asleep. I looked at my watch, and I had exactly thirty minutes to get to Dozier for services, and it was at least 25 minutes away.

The services at Dozier were a little different. There were almost 30 people there for my first sermon, and they had a choir and an organ. We sang some different songs, had some different announcements, but the sermon was exactly the same. I don't know who was more bored, them or me. But I had a whole row of youth on the back pew that gave me hope. That service came mercifully to a close, and I was invited out to lunch. My day was almost over. Just one sermon to go.

I looked at the schedule from the District Superintendent, and it said clearly that there was a 7:00 p.m. service at Cameron's Chapel on the first Sundays. So I left early so that I could get to the church about 6:30 p.m. I figured that I could greet everybody when they came in. Much to my surprise, the parking lot was filled and all of the lights were on when I arrived. "Did I miss a meeting or something?" were the first words out of my mouth.

"Almost," they said in unison.

"Was I given the wrong time for the service?"

"If you were given something other than 6:00 pm, you were."

I showed someone the sheet from the superintendent just to let her know I wasn't lying.

"We haven't met at 7:00 pm for over ten years."

"Well, let's sing a song or two."

"We already did."

"Let's have a time of prayer then…"

"We have."

"How about, I preach my sermon."

"I suggest you do that," said Miz Alberta, the only face I recognized in the whole place since she was at the meeting on Saturday.

I went to the pulpit, read the scripture, preached the same sermon I had preached twice already in the morning (amazing, the third time through it was almost memorized). And I left quickly that evening feeling lucky I was not strung up by a bunch of impatient Methodists.

Searight was scheduled for 9:30 am on that next Sunday, so I arrived there in plenty of time. There was an elderly woman playing the piano, and I guessed that she was my pianist. She welcomed me, and then asked me what I wanted to sing. I made a few suggestions, and each time she looked at me sort of strangely, and said, "I don't know that one." I looked through a hymnal and though I had never seen one like it before, I knew some of the music. I suggested a few more, and she kept saying, "I don't know that one either...If you sing a few lines, I can pick it up, but I can't read a note." So we found a couple of hymns she could play and we got ready for the service. At about 9:20 am, someone said, "Why don't you start preacher, everyone is here."

"Really, you don't wait till starting time?

"We really don't see the need. Everyone in town who's going to church has already made it to church."

So I started my first service at 9:25, and everybody was there. All twelve of them crammed into two rows in the front next to the piano. We finished up, visited a moment and I took off for Cameron's Chapel. I was not going to be 30 minutes late this Sunday.

...

Short Takes from that First Appointment

Have you ever had a house full of rats? The thought of that parsonage in Dozier still makes me queasy. I can take comfort knowing that I was not the one who brought them to the house. They were there before me, and they had set up housekeeping. They may have been the reason that my predecessor left in the middle of the night one December, but he never came back around to say.

I remember lying in bed on that first Saturday night, trying to get some rest for the next day, and the rats were in the kitchen playing in the pots and pans under the sink. I believe they were trying to cook one night when they knocked the big frying pan off the cupboard around two o'clock. Let's just say I was not rested that next morning when I gave my sermon at Oakey Streak.

I moved into that house in February, put food in the cabinets the first weekend, went back to college for a week, and when I returned the following Saturday, the rats had eaten everything they could get into. (Some of you are saying to yourselves, "Those weren't rats, they were mice." I say they left footprints that were larger than the average mouse's, and they had the ability to move things that most mice would not attempt—they were rats if not bigger vermin that infested my kitchen).

That weekend I began to clean up the mess, and the following weekend washed the entire cabinets down and laid out poison. They appeared to leave when I would arrive on Saturday morning, but every time I put food in the cabinets, I would have trouble. They knew I would be gone every Sunday evening, and they would bring the party back to my kitchen.

This went on every weekend until the summer, when I moved into the house full-time. I had a quest, and it was to rid that house of those nasty creatures. I cleaned out cabinets, closets, and any nook or cranny where a rat might hide. I put out traps and poison, and kept a long stick handy to beat them senseless. I cut the grass real short and cleaned up the shrubbery around the house and made the house look and feel like a home. I only caught one rat in a trap, and from the smell of it, a couple died under the house. Over the first month of the summer, the rats just gave up and gave me back the house. I rested well on Saturday nights once again.

...

One of the joys and pitfalls of being a preacher in the rural south is that when vegetable season arrives, so do the bags of surplus vegetables on your porch. I don't think it occurred to anyone that I was single, and did not know how to freeze and can vegetables. I would wake up in the morning and there would be a bag of peas and a watermelon. I would go to the store, and come back and there would be a half-bushel of tomatoes. Later in the day, somebody would bring squash or cucumbers. All of these vegetables were brought in the kind of quantities that a family of eight might eat, and I was by myself most every night. I ate so many tomato sandwiches that summer in Dozier that my mouth was sore from all of the acid. I became a vegetarian that summer, because I really didn't have time to cook meat, since I had so many vegetables to learn to prepare.

What I didn't eat myself, I gave away, which is pretty hard when everybody has more than enough in their own gardens. I would visit a shut-in, try and share my tomatoes or peas, and she would show me that I was already too late. There were bags full of produce sitting on her kitchen floor. "Can you pass some of these along to someone who needs them?"

Early in the summer, I would be nice and try to get rid of the extras for them. Later in the summer, it was too much work. I hate to admit it, but on many occasions I just took the vegetables straight from the porch to the compost heap I started in the back yard. That was just how the seasonal glut of vegetables worked.

When watermelons started coming in, it was a great pleasure to get one on the porch at the end of the week. I love watermelon, and I could eat it by the pound. It was a great treat on a Friday or Saturday night. But as the season matured, they started showing up every day. They would make sure that I was gone, and drop one in front of the door. One day I had three sitting in front of the door when I returned from the hospital. A man can only eat so much watermelon. My digestive track can attest to that fact.

I heard through the grapevine that the barrage of watermelons was masterminded by one of the cantankerous old men of the community. He wanted to see how long it would take for the young preacher to break down and ask people to quit sending watermelons from the pulpit. I decided to develop a counter plan of my own.

Tip was the mailman in town and was a brother-in-law to Lowell, my watermelon friend, and he enjoyed nothing better than a practical joke. I stockpiled watermelons for a week, and I kept them stacked in the cool room of the house so they wouldn't get mushy. Then on a Thursday night, when we knew the Lions Club was meeting, and knew that Lowell would be out of the house for a few hours, Tip came to the house with his pick-up and we loaded fifteen large watermelons into the back of his truck. We drove up to Lowell's house and stacked them in front of his door.

The story goes that Lowell had to go to the bathroom bad before he left the Lion's Club meeting, but preferred to go at the house than at the high school cafeteria. When he drove up and saw the door blocked, he began to be concerned that he could not move the watermelons and take care of business. Lowell told Tip when he delivered the mail the next day that he "had to sh**t in the woods because of that g**d** preacher." Tip never let on that he was involved.

I never got another watermelon that summer.

...

Dozier was a small, sleepy Southern town in 1981. Though the civil rights movement came through town long before, and the school had integrated in 1972, there was still a great divide between blacks and whites in that community when I served there. I would not doubt that over twenty years later, there is still a basic divide in that community over race.

I was just twenty years old at the time, and I was still young, naïve and idealistic. I believed that the divide that most of the Deep South created was artificial, and that there was no reason to live in hatred and bigotry. My roommate at college was black, and some of my best friends were black, and it didn't occur to me that this could still be a problem.

At the Dozier school, I developed a friendship with one of the teachers on staff. He taught English through the week, and preached every Sunday at a black, Baptist Church down the road. He was a genuinely good teacher, had the student's best interest at heart, and wanted to do all that he could to offer the Gospel in the place where he lived and taught.

One afternoon in the spring as we were talking, we got this idea. There were over 100 kids in school, but the combined number of kids in church on a Sunday morning in Dozier might have been 30. We reasoned that the largest portion of kids would probably never set foot in a local church, but might come to the school if something were offered. We cooked up this plan to have a Christian day camp in late June, get the school to host it (the principal was a member of my church, and really didn't care what the Supreme Court said about separation of Church and State), and we would provide a program for all of the kids of the community.

I had some parents that were interested at my church, he had some at his church, and we thought that maybe the Baptist Church in town would consider the idea and provide some staff and money. What I discovered was that this was an idea that was way beyond its time. The pastor at the Baptist Church did not resort to wild profanity, but came very close to exploding on his front porch when I brought up the idea. "What kind of n***r loving preacher are you?" Once I heard the "N" word, I knew that there would be no reasonable discussion to follow, so I just left him and said, "I am sorry you feel that way."

The next week was quite an eye opener. One of my members let me know that there would be a Ku Klux Klan meeting on Friday night, the first one in years. He suggested that maybe I would go to Montgomery for the evening. Before I even heard the news, I had made plans to meet up with a friend and go out to dinner. So it was really no problem. When I got back late that night, there were cars parked about a block from the house and you could tell that there was drinking and rowdiness going on. I thought twice about getting out of the car and going in the house, but I did. About 15 minutes later, about 10 cars drove by the house real slowly, revving their engines. They circled back a few times and then left. I was even more wide-awake that night than when the rats knocked the pan off the cupboard.

The next morning when I walked down to the post office, a group of men shouted something derogatory at me as I walked past. I didn't hear what they said, but I knew I better not reply so I kept walking. The following day, we were missing a few people in church that were normally there. There was a bit of tension that I hadn't recognized before. I wondered how many of my membership had been at the Klan meeting on Friday night.

Things continued tensely for the next week, and usually every night around eleven o'clock. There would be several cars that would make circles around the block, and you could tell the drivers were glaring at me as they drove by. I tried to live as normally as possible, but I began locking doors more frequently and locking up my car at night, and inspecting everything that came to the porch.

The last week of school was coming up, and I was asked months before to preach the baccalaureate sermon in the high school auditorium. It was the only Sunday of the year that all of the churches of the community closed services and went to church together. The whole community turned up to honor the nine graduating seniors of Dozier High School. There were two seniors from my church, two from the Baptist church, and the other five from the black congregations in the surrounding area. It was a fascinating gathering like I had not experienced before in that community.

I preached on the theme: "Living Out Your Dreams" and preached roughly from a portion of Genesis where Joseph interpreted the dreams of Pharaoh, and I quoted the title of Martin Luther King Jr.'s famous sermon, "I Have a

Dream." Overall, it was a pretty benign sermon about living up to your potential and having high expectations--the kind of speech that they had already heard plenty of. And yet, unknowingly my choice of words cut some people to the core. Halfway through my sermon, the Baptist preacher and a number of his congregation walked out. I learned the power of the spoken word that day.

My English teacher friend told me that I had done a bold thing that morning, and all I could think was that it shouldn't be thought of as bold, because it was 1981 and not 1951. That sermon essentially put an end to any thought of a day camp, and kept the Klan stirring for a few more weeks.

Late one night after the Klan circled slowly by the house, I got a phone call from my college roommate. As soon as I picked up the phone, I heard the words: "I ought to kill you boy…" but had no clue who was on the other end. I slammed down the receiver, turned off all the lights in the house, and lay down on the floor. The phone rang again, and it was a familiar voice, "What is going on down there?" I explained to him what had been going on in Dozier while he was in Wetumpka for the summer.

"I am sorry about the 'ought to kill you' business. I just hadn't heard from you since college let out, and wanted to know how things are going."

"Well, now you know."

"You need to lay low for awhile. The Klan has been known to kill folks, you know?" (Some of his own family in earlier years to be exact.)

"I'm just trying to be faithful."

"Faithful can get you killed…be careful down there."

"I'll try."

I hung up the phone and remained wide-awake for several hours lying on the floor in the dark.

…

The Klan scared me that summer, but probably the most dangerous thing about my job was driving the back roads of rural Alabama. Many of my church members lived on dirt roads way off the beaten track, and to make a visit was taking your life in your hands. When it was raining, the red clay of South

Alabama was as slick as pigeon poop, and on more than one occasion I found myself sliding through stop signs at intersections, or putting the car into a spin or a slide trying to avoid dogs or stray cattle.

The paved roads were even more dangerous because they gave you the idea that you could drive at a normal speed, only to top a hill and nearly hit a tractor on its way to the field. The paved roads also gave you the impression that there were two lanes of traffic, but in actuality, there was only room for a large pickup truck to go one way (and that was the normal means of transportation around Dozier).

The other transportation factor that was always an issue was Sunday mornings. I never had problems on first and third Sundays, because it was only about eight miles between Searight and Cameron's Chapel. If services ended at 10:30 a.m. at Searight, I could be at Cameron's Chapel by 10:45 a.m. On the other hand, it was 25 minutes of hard driving from Oakey Streak back to the church in Dozier. If I happened to get out late, there was no way to get to the other church on time. I always planned to arrive early at Oakey Streak so that I could visit and catch up on the news before service, so that I could head straight out the door after the benediction. Occasionally, there would be problems.

I will never forget the Sunday we had communion, and the service went a little long. I looked at my watch and I was finishing the service at exactly 10:30 am. By the time I could get out the door, into the car, and out the driveway, I knew that I would have to hurry to get to Dozier to set up for communion there. I made a snap decision to leave my robe on to drive. It was a white alb with a rope belt. It was stylish for rural Alabama at the time. I figured that decision would save me a couple of minutes on either end of the trip.

On the way out to the main road, I got behind a little old couple headed to their church, and I couldn't pass. Time was wasting. I finally got to the Georgianna highway, and knew that I would have to do something drastic to get to the other church on time. I floored the accelerator and watched the speedometer inch glide past 55, to 65, 75, then to 85. When the car reached 90 miles per hours I was topping a hill, only to meet a State Trooper coming up the other side. His light blinked once, and I hit the brakes, and pulled to the side. I got out of the car, forgetting that I had my robe on, and walked back to get my ticket.

He never started writing in his book, he just laughed, "Do you have some kind of Jesus thing going or what?"

"To tell you the truth I do."

I explained to him my predicament, and how I was late, and it was communion Sunday, and he just shook his head and said, "Then you better get back on the road...You've got some folks praying for you this morning. Slow it down now, you hear?"

I arrived in Dozier, about five minutes after the hour. The organist was playing the prelude, and somebody had done the announcements, they had been through this before. As I walked to the pulpit one of my leaders asked jokingly if the law had gotten me.

I replied, "If you only knew."

The Camp Director

Since I was in junior high, I have usually gone to camp, or on a church retreat, or spent a portion of the summer outdoors. This has been going on almost thirty years now, and for the most part, I look forward to the opportunity. While I was in college I had this dream of maybe being a full-time camp director and living my life on retreat and in the outdoors. There is nothing like doing it full-time to squelch that enthusiasm.

I was twenty–three years old and I let someone talk me into the possibility of becoming a camp director. I can say that it was a vulnerable time in my life. I had four years of college and two years of seminary under my belt, and I was tired of school. I was also restless about the idea of what I was going to do when I finished seminary. Would I continue on to school? Would I get a job in the church? Could I do something else? All of these questions led me to agree to apply for the job of camp director, at a little camp named Bobwhite (in memory of a guy named "Bob White"), which was supposed to remind you of the quail. I discovered that I was the only applicant and that they only went through the formalities of the interview to see if I was mentally deranged. After all, this camp was isolated if not a very primitive situation. It would take a special kind of person that could live there year-round.

Camp Bobwhite is located in the foothills of North Carolina. On the map it doesn't look that far from Charlotte, but the map will only fool you. The camp was located about a mile down a dirt road, about seven miles off of anything that would remind you of a major highway. My mailbox was ten miles from the house, and the nearest chain grocery store was twenty-four miles away. I had neighbors that were pretty close by foot, but quite a long way by car. A majority of the year, about forty-four weeks to be exact, the camp was fairly empty, except for the guests who came on weekends. For five days a week I was left with the quiet of the woods, some fish ponds and open land. Two days a week were filled with the sounds of adults, children and youth that had come for a weekend away.

Seven days a week I lived in a mobile home that appeared to be abandoned on the property twenty years before. It was burning hot in the summer and ice cold in the winter. Every spring the rains would pour in from the tiny holes in the roof and siding, and every fall the field mice and snakes would pour in the cracks and holes in the floor seeking warmth from the impending winter. Living in the trailer was like camping year round, except the ground was usually cleaner.

The job consisted of managing over 100 acres of land, cutting about 15 acres of grass, caring for a lodge that would hold 60 people, and scheduling groups and camps for the entire year. I was also responsible for helping to raise funds, build new facilities, and do public relations for the camp. I did all of this for $10,000 dollars, the opportunity to live in the trailer, and health insurance. As a single guy with almost no expenses, it was a pretty good job. I looked at other camp directors doing similar jobs, and I knew I was being used, but it was my choice to be taken advantage of, so I have no one to blame but myself.

I was actually the first camp director that Bobwhite ever had. In its twenty-year history, the director was usually a local pastor that was given the task of managing schedule and calendar. They hired out custodians and grass cutting. Anything else done at or for the camp was purely volunteer. I discovered that by paying me money to do the job, they effectively fired a half-dozen people that were doing bits and pieces of the job, making me the new local schmuck.

Because I had a committee that hired me and a board that paid my bills, I had then become answerable to the whims and fancies of a dozen people who thought they knew the job better than I did, and had no intentions of ever lifting the proverbial finger to get the job done. What a learning experience for a young adult.

My first experience of how this worked was when I arrived on the job the first week of May. The chair of the committee told me that one of the first things I needed to do was order fertilizer for the grass. They prided themselves on having some of the grassiest fields in the camping industry. When I drove up on the property, I was assured they had grass. It was about two feet tall and had not been cut all spring. I suggested that fertilizer was the least of the camp's needs---some serious grass cutting was the first thing on the agenda. The chair of the committee took offense, and ordered the fertilizer himself. I found it amusing to be on the tractor for the third solid day cutting grass while the fertilizer truck dropped a couple of tons of fertilizer on the fields.

During the second week, I got a call from the treasurer asking why I had ordered fertilizer on my first day of work, I explained that I didn't order the fertilizer. He said that Mr. White (the father of the deceased Bob of

"Bobwhite") had already spread two tons of fertilizer a month earlier.   I told the treasurer I was sorry, but I had nothing to do with either of those actions, and that I was doing my best just to keep the grass cut. Let's just say that we could have gotten a major award for having the healthiest grass at a camp in the state.

After being the director for about a month, one of my board members showed up with a horse trailer and tells me to come with her to pick up a pony, "Every camp needs a pony," were her very words.   I tried to reason with her that this was not a great idea, and that it was much more trouble than the camp needed, and her response was, "Remember that we can fire you as easily as we hired you."

So I went to get the pony as a means of keeping my job. It was a cute pony, but mean as could be. He would bite you if you turned your head, and he would kick if you got near his hindquarters, all the while the old guy who was selling the pony dirt-cheap kept saying, "He's the most gentle thing you'll ever put a harness on." Seems this pony was not the riding kind, but the cart-pulling kind. The board member paid for the pony, and the tack and harnesses and the cart, and was getting a receipt so that she could get a tax deduction for donating it to the camp. I could see the old man smiling. He knew that he had taken a city slicker, and he shed his life of a cantankerous pony. I asked him what he called the pony, and he replied, "Buckshot."

When it came time to put the pony on the trailer, the pony had other intentions. The old man let the board member know that the pony had never ridden in a trailer in its life. He wished us the best and went on in the house with his money. The pony sat on his backside refusing to get up. The board member beat Buckshot with a leather strap, while I pulled on his halter. The pony did not budge. We decided to try and coax the animal into the trailer with food, and the pony lay on its side. The board member made a phone call and brought in reinforcements, and two of her husband's friends came to help. Between the four of us, we slid the pony a couple of feet toward the trailer on its side. Out of frustration, this prim and proper lady from the city who had just lain down a few hundred dollars began cussing the pony out with words I had never heard before coming out of a woman's mouth. Almost immediately the pony stood up and walked into the trailer. It finally heard words it understood. I thought how bad it would sound for the camp director to cuss out the pony in front of a bunch of campers. I figured with or without the pony, I had a good chance of losing my job that summer.

...

Before the summer camp season began, I discovered ways to get free help. I had painting to be done, and no time to do it. I had firewood for the winter to cut, and yet the mower had to be operating nearly every day to keep up with the grass. So I went to the county offices to see what was available. There was a program for underprivileged youth that needed to place a few local boys into gainful employment. They would pay all their wages; all I had to do was supervise them 20 hours per week. What problem could that be? The other program was community service for persons who were first time offenders of the state's driving while intoxicated laws. They said they had a guy who would be perfect for the job who needed to work off about forty hours in the next two months. I was ecstatic.

The next Saturday, my DWI guy showed, and he was everything I didn't hope for. He was a slick talker who really didn't want to work. He was a know-it-all that knew he was beyond menial labor. He complained that the paint I gave him for the porch was not the right kind of paint, and I explained to him that it was the same paint that had been used for the past ten years. When I asked him to fix the toilet, he said that the entire bathroom needed reworking and he had a friend that could do it real cheap. I just about lost it when he told me that the axe I gave him to split wood was not balanced and that no one could split wood with it. I proceeded to show him that I must be just the right amount off-balance since I could split a log with one whack three times in a row. I suggested that he try a little work before he said another word. I calculated that the first six hours he worked in community service, cost me about eight hours of my time in supervision and redoing his mistakes.

The next Saturday, he showed up and told me how much he looked forward to coming to the camp all week. He said he liked the peace and quiet, and how he believed hard work was good for the soul. I thought to myself that his soul was in need of repair based on the week before. It just so happens that there was a retreat group in for the weekend, and I asked the guy to stay out of their way.

His community service agreement stated plainly that he was not to "consort or associate with the general public" while he worked off his hours. I had him painting in a downstairs bathroom while I was trimming the ditches with a weed eater. I was gone for no more than thirty minutes, and I found him up next to the women's dorm pretending to fix a door that had nothing wrong with it. I asked him what he thought he was doing and he offered the excuse, "One of those girls asked me to come up and fix the door."

"Have you finished your painting downstairs?"
"No."
"Think you might today?"
"Probably not, the roller you gave me is the wrong kind."
"I suggest you figure out how to use it, since the professional who donated the materials thought it was just the right thing. Humor me, please. Do some work."

I went back to the ditches, and about thirty minutes later I caught him not only talking to a teenager that was there with her church group, I caught him saying something suggestive about how balanced her bosoms and backside were. It was at that point that I told him to start walking to the highway, and that I would call his wife to pick him up at the camp gate. He asked, "What did I do wrong?" I suggested he had about a mile of walking to think about it. His last words to me were, "Do you want me to come back next Saturday?"

The underprivileged youth were not much better. They were teenagers, so I could forgive their laziness and foul language a little easier, but it still got under my skin that I had to spend so much time supervising and correcting their work. Not to mention, fixing the tractor, the truck and a number of other pieces of equipment they managed to beat up over the summer. The only job they seemed to excel at was stacking firewood. So every afternoon when their four hours ended, I would go and find dead trees to cut up into firewood, and devise a plan so that they had to stack it forty or fifty yards away, and they could only use a wheel barrow to transport it (since the truck was off limits after they hit a tree with it). It was busy work, and not very creative, but if you had met these boys, you would have done the same thing. Creativity was not in their future.

One morning I had given them another job to do. They were supposed to drag limbs; vines and other trash down to a gully just a couple hundred yards from my trailer. They were gone a long time, so I went looking for them, and found them with their hands up in the air and my drunk and crazy neighbor waving a pistol at them.

"Whoa Eugene, what are you doing to my summer help?" was my first anxious question.

"They were trespassing on my property, and I aim to either have them arrested or kill them."

"Well killing them will only get you in trouble, and I don't think the sheriff will arrest them."

"They're on my land."

"Yeah, but you said that I could put the trash in your gully anytime I wanted to."

"These guys ain't you."

"You've got me there, but I don't think the sheriff will look at your threatening to kill them over a bit of trash as a good thing."

"You may have got me there."

"You gonna put down the gun and let them go back to the camp?"
"I reckon I better."

"Thanks."

The boys kept coming to work every day, and I was surprised that it was possible. If they told their supervisor, I am sure that they would have been sent somewhere else based on safety concerns. Knowing those boys, they probably thought it was cool to be working at a job for minimum wage that brought with it so much danger. All I can say is that I was glad when they went back to school in the fall, and I didn't have to cut so much firewood.

. . .

After the campers left for the summer, and the weather began getting crisp, campers only came on the weekends. Cool weather meant hunting season, as well as moonshine season. Living back on a dirt road like mine, wild game was plentiful. It was not uncommon to see deer, turkey, fox and raccoon all in one trip to the main road. With that knowledge came the hunters. Most nights during raccoon season, there would be someone running dogs on camp property. I was not happy with it, but I had learned the community well enough to know that you don't cross hunters with shotguns. So I made friends with them. I would go out and stand by the truck with them, listen to dogs on the chase, and then be sure to remind them that campers were coming in on Friday afternoon, and it scares the little ones when they run the dogs at night. They were very helpful, and never hunted when campers were on the premises.

I never let them know that it scared the heck out of me that guys who may have had too much to drink were walking around the property with loaded weapons. I was grateful that there was an actual hunting season that kept their habits to a minimum and that for the most part these were law-abiding citizens.

The moon shiners were a different story. There were several in the community, and something told me that my crazy neighbor down the road was in cahoots with them. Maybe it was the large amounts of sugar he kept stored in his barn or the huge amounts of corn that he ordered each week for his 20 or so chickens that roamed his yard.

I never ventured in the woods beyond the camp property because I did not want to find anything I would have to lie about or keep secret. But I knew that it was going on because Otis Hudson told me so.

Otis showed up one November morning on my doorstep with a quart jar in his hand. He explained that he came from a long line of Hudson's that were moon shiners in the area, but he had discovered a way to do it legally.

"Legally?" I asked.

"Because I don't sell it, I have done nothing wrong."

"So you can make moonshine legally?"

He explained to me laws that I had never heard of before, and have never bothered to verify, but he was quite convincing. "As long as you don't make over 200 gallons, and only share it with family or friends, it is perfectly legal. You are now a friend," he smiled as he handed me a quart jar of clear liquid.

"I won't get in trouble having it in my house?"

"You didn't pay for it did you?"

"No."

"So you aren't breaking any laws. Don't be driving while drinking it though, that could get you in trouble."

"I'll try to remember that."

Otis went on to explain how he made a living with legal moonshine. "You see, I am what some people think of as a folk treasure. I have skills that are going out of style, and people will actually pay you to show off those skills."

"Naw, you're kidding me."
"Really, I leave tomorrow for a county fair, and come back and teach at the junior college next week."

"Teach what?"

"Mountain living. Those college kids eat up everything about my still, and how we make moonshine, and how we avoided the law for all those years."

"People pay you to show them how your still works?"
"Yep, ain't that a kick. And as long as I don't sell the stuff, I am perfectly legal."

"That's a kick all right."

So every couple of months, I found a quart jar of Otis Hudson's "white lightning" beside the back door. I followed all of Otis' directions for mountain remedies. Honey and peppermint soaked in grain alcohol makes a great cough syrup. Eating one or two raisins soaked in corn liquor each day was good for lower back pain. He recommended washing my face every week with moonshine on a cotton ball to keep pores clean (it cleaned better than any store bought astringent that you pay ten bucks for). It was a little too strong to drink straight, but I had a friend that mixed it with Kool Aid who relieved me of nearly every jar that ended up on my porch. I look back through my life, and Otis Hudson may have been one of my most generous friends.

. . .

A man's best friend is his dog. Being the director at Bobwhite gave me the chance to have a best friend. When you live a mile off the beaten track, animals have this funny way of showing up. One month would be cats, and the next month puppies. Early on the pony showed up on the property. Geese and ducks appeared later. Beyond it being a camp for people, it was retreat or hostel for animals.

I obtained my dog "Buck" because someone wanted a good home for his dog. Buck was a purebred Alaskan husky, had the looks of a wolf, but was as gentle with humans as any cat I had ever had. Yet his gentleness with humans hid his predilection for eating other animals. Buck had to be sent further into the country because he had a bad habit of chasing cows. He had yet to hurt one, but his former owner was being bullied by his cattle raising neighbors to kill the dog. Sending him to camp was what his former owner thought would be a solution.

He was great with kids. He would lie out on the porch all day just waiting to be rubbed. The campers would tie bandannas around his neck, put bows in his hair, and even make him wear t-shirts and gym shorts. Amazingly, Buck would hang around all day and take the abuse. As long as campers were on the premises, he was a social animal, and I never had to worry about him.

When the campers left, and Buck had too much free time, he became a nuisance. He and the pony would fight nearly every day. Buck would attempt to bite the pony in the neck, and the pony would swing around and kick Buck with his hind legs. On more than one occasion I saw Buck knocked out cold and lying in the pasture. I figured that the pony was safe.

The other animals on the property were not safe. The cats cut country and had no intentions of being eaten by a dog. The ducks flew off, never to be heard from again. The geese were not so lucky. Their flying feathers were removed, so all they could do was swim in the pond. Buck had a feast around Thanksgiving time.

I came back from the post office one afternoon, and noticed feathers scattered from the pond to my trailer. I knew this was not good, and I was prepared for the worst. The male goose had been killed, chewed on and left for dead in my back yard. I hit Buck a few times with a stick in view of the carcass, and yelled at him about taking the life of an easygoing animal (after all there were all kinds of wild animals that would have been better sport, and made the camp a much better place). I knew that this was not going to be helpful, but it made me feel better. Then I got a shovel and buried the goose out near my garden.

The next day, I came home from the post office and Buck had dug up the goose and chewed on him some more. I reburied the goose, and it happened again. For five days this went on, and on the sixth day, Buck could hardly stand. He had this sick look on his face, and I immediately diagnosed him as having eaten too much rancid goose.

I had a few options to weigh. Would I let nature take its course, or take Buck to the local veterinarian? I knew that if I took him to the vet, I would have to get the dog tagged, registered and then go through the hassle of shots and de-worming. It would have cost a fortune to go that direction, so I opted for letting nature take its course. After all, what dog has not eaten something rancid in its life?

The next day, Buck looked really bad. He had a pale look to him, even though his hair was dark around the face. It was the eyes that gave him away, and they kept looking into my eyes—"Do something!"

When I went to town, I stopped by a country store and picked up a bottle of the remedy that always worked for me. Though there has never been any scientific proof that castor oil has healing properties, I know that when I took it, I could will my way into wellness so that I wouldn't have to take a second dose.

That afternoon when I got home Buck looked pitiful. He had not moved off the porch all afternoon, and he had this low whimper that cried out pain. I took the bottle out of the bag, opened the top and proceeded to get about 4 ounces down his throat. He was not at all happy with me, but too weak to fight or run, so I poured the rest of the 8-ounce bottle in his mouth.

That sick look in his eyes became a glazed one, and he began to look like he was really in pain. I put him in the back of the pick-up truck and I drove to a friend's house to get a second opinion and maybe a recommendation for a good veterinarian. Buck never moved out of the truck, which was pretty strange. Usually Buck would chase their dog around the yard, or wander over to the pasture to chase cows. They knew Buck was sick and suggested I take him to the vet first thing in the morning. "See if the castor oil works, and if he's still sick, get him to the vet." I drove home, and Buck remained in the back of the truck. I wondered if he would still be alive in the morning when I went to bed.

The next morning I heard barking outside the window. I looked and Buck was chasing a squirrel across the yard. I went out on the porch and he came up wagging his tail, and you knew if dogs smiled, he had a large grin on his face. He ate a bowl of dog food early that day, and looked famished for some more.

I chalked that cure up to castor oil and the belief that even the worst of things pass through the end.

The Professional Student

I finished high school in Alabama in a class of seventy-two students. Of that group, maybe half went on to get further education of some kind. Of that half, maybe half completed a four-year degree, or about 25% of the total class (which is a pretty large percentage considering that region of the country). Of the eighteen or so people who completed a bachelor's degree, maybe six or eight went on to get their master's degree. At my last reunion, which was my twentieth, I was the only one who completed a Ph.D. That degree and a dollar may get a cup of coffee in some places, but it is a tribute to the fact that I once had a career as a professional student.

I can truly say that I enjoyed going to school. There were not many days or classes I didn't look forward to. That is the only explanation I have for being able to endure, not just four years of college, and four years of Master's work, but what amounted to nine years of enrollment for my Ph.D. True story: when I went to get a marriage license in 1985, there was a line on the application that asked: "How many years have you been to school?" The largest number that you could check in the field was sixteen (twelve years of secondary plus four years of undergraduate). I had to use the fill-in-the-blank and write in 19. I calculated that if I had to fill that form out again, I would have to say—twenty-nine.

The first eight years of higher education I could not call professional. Professional implies that you might actually make some money doing something. Scholarships and the folks paid for my first four years of college. It was a fairly easy existence, and took very little income on my part to remain a student. In fact, most of the income that I did make was saved for future study.

The next four years were primarily my responsibility, and because of scholarships, some financial aid, a loan and summer internships, I was able to pay my way through four more years of school. It was not until my next degree that I became a professional.

The story of how I became a Ph.D. student is a pretty good story in itself. While I was still a college student I had this long-term dream of becoming a professor, possibly a professor of Old Testament /Hebrew Bible. I worked the angles carefully. I made sure that I took Hebrew and German. I knew that in order to get through a Ph.D. in Old Testament I would still have to learn Greek and French, and possibly another dead language. I was ready to fulfill all of those requirements when I made application to a graduate school.

By that time I was married, and I had made promises that we would move to Washington, DC so that my wife Diane could finish her master's program. There was only one school in the area that had an Old Testament department that I cared to enter, and that was Catholic University. So I only made application there.

It was an exciting day when I received word that I was accepted to begin in fall 1986. There was even a brief handwritten note from an advisor who said he was excited to have a United Methodist clergy in the program. I was told that I needed to have an onsite interview sometime in the spring, so I put that plan in motion for my spring break.

I arrived at the Catholic University campus, had my interview with a well-known Old Testament scholar from the Catholic tradition. He was pleased with my grades at Duke, he knew that my skills in Hebrew were adequate, my German should be fine, and he was confident that I could learn the other languages in the mandatory five years. He shook my hand welcomed me to the department, and then handed me an outline of fees required by September.

I couldn't believe my eyes when I saw the figure at the bottom—roughly $20,000 dollars.

"Who do I need to speak to about financial aid?" was the next question out of my mouth.

"We don't have an office of financial aid."

"Then you must have some sort of program for teaching or research assistants that I can be involved with."
"No, all of our students are full-time students."

My heart fell below my belt and I was feeling very sick. I had managed to go through eight years of higher education and was only in about $2,000 dollars debt, and most of that was a service loan that I wouldn't have to pay back if I gave the church a couple of years of service. Now I was faced with a bill for one year of $20,000 dollars.

When Diane and I talked that night, my desire to get a Ph.D. had diminished thoroughly. I calculated that it would take three to four years to complete the degree, which would mean roughly $60,000-80,000 in debt. That fact coupled with the fact that there were usually 50-60 applications for every job in Old Testament across the country, and my desire to pursue that degree became smaller. I imagined having a degree, an outrageous loan to repay, and not being able to get a job. I began to start thinking creatively.

I had about twenty-four hours in Washington before I had to return to North Carolina, so I drove to the nearest State University—The University of Maryland. It was just a couple of miles from Washington, DC and not far from where we knew we would be living in September.

I went to admissions, got a catalogue, and began thumbing through the pages for a degree program that might take me, and that I might want to pursue. It came down to two departments—agriculture and recreation. I considered agriculture because of my rural background, and I still had a misplaced dream of making a living from the land. Recreation was an option because I had spent several summers and a couple of years working in church camps, and thought that I might be able to develop a course of study in church recreation.

I discovered quickly that a degree in theology was not an adequate prerequisite for studying agriculture. There is this assumption that those students will show a firm grasp of math and sciences, not exegesis and liturgy. So I was down to one department.

I made a brief appointment with the chair of the department for the next morning and told him what I was thinking of doing, and he asked me to complete my application and I would get special treatment. I understood later that everyone who showed interest in the department got special treatment. They took every student that applied for graduate studies, because they needed a quota to receive university funds. I helped make their fall semester a possibility. Therefore, I was treated well.

A month later I came back to campus with my letter of acceptance and talked with my advisor. He informed me that I would have to pay for my first semester of school, but that if I were patient, my troubles would be solved. I looked at the fees due in September ($2,000 dollars) and compared it to Catholic University ($20,000 dollars) and immediately thought—"I can do this."

I arrived at the University about a month before classes started. I knew that I had to secure some employment to make expenses, so I began to look through job postings all over campus. Most jobs were paying minimum wage, and those that paid a little better needed skills I didn't have. I went to the school of agriculture and told a secretary my situation and background, and she said, "Wait right here."

In a few minutes a guy not much older than me with "Dr." in front of his name came down stairs and introduced himself as the head of a project in the department of entomology. "It's not exciting work, but the pay's good."

I discovered this massive research project on Gypsy Moths that was short of bodies. The job would entail everything from raising gypsy moth larvae to field collection and counting of moths. When that project was slow, I could work with a hornworm eradication program, which involved raising tobacco and worms and killing them both. As I became better known in the department, I was asked to help edit papers and books, and was trusted with a portion of the 'armored scales project."

It was always a hilarious experience to explain how a guy with a degree in theology was working with a bunch of entomologists. When Gary Larson, the entomologist who became the world-renowned cartoonist of 'Far Side' fame came to town, they made sure I was introduced. They figured that Larson would get a kick out of a divinity student counting dead Gypsy Moths for a living.

I spent my first semester of school between the Colleges of Agriculture and the College of Health and Human Performance. In one I studied, in the other I killed insects, or counted dead ones. It was a fascinating existence.

When classes started in January, I moved from amateur to professional status as a student. The package I received from the university was very generous. In return for assisting with research and teaching with a professor, I would have all of my classes paid for, and receive a salary of $7,500 dollars per year. Plus I got health insurance and some other university benefits. It came out to about fifteen hours work per week, with nine hours of classes, and I was getting paid for it. What a deal.

Over the two and a half years I was with that department I lectured on special topics, graded papers and read essays, assisted with research projects, and even taught a few classes of my own. One summer I was given the title, "Assistant Director" for the Wildland Conservation and Resources Planning School, which was a six-week special program, held in the mountains of New Hampshire. That meant that I did everything that the director didn't want to do. That meant teach for two of the six weeks, go on all of the hiking and overnight trips, deal with student discipline, and even deal with university administration for all of the mistakes that the director made. In exchange for the title, I was given one-third tuition remission for enrolling in the program. When a grad student that was supposed to teach for two weeks dropped out, and I had to take over her duties, the director saw to it that I would get none of her tuition reimbursement. Instead, he said, "I'll take care of you next fall."

Next fall came, and the director decided he would take a leave of absence from the department. He had used his summer in New Hampshire to locate a job closer to his wife, so my compensation was that I was given one of his classes that he dropped in the department's lap, along with the class I was already scheduled to teach—all at the same pay. (What a deal!) I dropped the guy as an advisor and it was a move that made the rest of my days at the University of Maryland more enjoyable.

For all but a few months of the rest of my time in residence, I taught courses of my own and contributed to research that gave me publications and great experiences. I even had my brush with fame and fortune while teaching.

I had a survey course that met three days a week at 9:00 a.m. Sitting on the front row most days was the starting quarterback for the university football team, who would later become a first round draft choice in the NFL. Neil O'Donnell was a bright guy, and it concerned me that test after test he was just getting by with a "C". I asked him once why he didn't want to do better than a "C," and his reply was this: "Man, in a few months I'm going to sign a contract for a few million dollars, and I am going to make over a million a year. In a few months you will still be teaching this course making a teacher's assistant salary. Do you think it really matters to me?" Point taken. Neil went on to play for several years, and I believe he's now selling cars in New Jersey. I figure I might make my first million by the time I retire.

I had another student that was a harder case than Neil. He was an All-American lacrosse player, who was not bright, and could not breeze by in my classes. He tried to make it on charm, but that kept getting in the way of his test scores, and the fact that he missed over half the classes. It was obvious at midterm that he had not read any of the assignments, and had not studied a lick when he had the lowest score ever made on one of my exams.

(True story: I gave a small group of students who had never heard one of my lectures before, or seen the material, and by pure logic, each scored higher than my lacrosse player.)

When an athlete did poorly on an exam, it usually meant a visit from academic services. They would research why the student did poorly, how he or she could improve, and what sort of steps could be made to pass the class. The explanation was pretty easy, he rarely came to class, he didn't read the assignments, and he did not use the brain God had given him. The tutor shook his head knowingly; he had heard this story before.

The lacrosse guy performed better on the second exam, making it possible for him to pass the course with a decent score on the final. But unfortunately, he handed in his final after about 20 minutes, and I knew it meant another visit from academic services.

This time it was the supervisor of his program meeting my department chair. Then I had the meeting we all hated. The "no pressure" meeting, that usually means that there was pressure involved.

"I won't make you do anything. You do what is right."
"So what do they want me to do?"

"Give him another shot at the exam."

"It will take a miracle for him to score high enough to pass."

"This is the athletic department; they believe in miracles."

"How about all of the other students that don't have an athletic department behind them, should I give them another chance?"

"I won't tell you what to do. I just know they are trying to save an All-American's scholarship."

I thought about it awhile, and called the student-athlete up. I told him to come prepared to take the exam 48 hours from the phone call. He thanked me, and I am certain he went immediately to his tutor and they began cramming a whole semester of class work into those two days. He arrived in my office a few minutes before the designated time looking like he had neither slept nor bathed in two days. I told him I would fax his grade over to academic services before five o'clock that day.

I calculated that he needed to get no less than 35 right out of 48 questions to pass the course. He scored a 36, and I sent a big letter "D" to academic services. That next year I watched this same guy score a couple of goals in the national championships courtesy of a soft-hearted teacher and a miracle.

My Career in Television

I am not sure what constitutes a career. The time I spent working in television was rather short, but an informative time in my life. Compared to others in the field, just over two years is a fairly long time. And for me, it was long enough.

I got into television through the back door. I knew someone who knew someone, and the rest is history. The person that I knew was a friend and classmate at the University of Maryland. We both entered the Ph.D. program in the Department of Recreation that same fall in 1986. We first met because we both had to take the same "remedial" class in research writing that was designed for undergraduate seniors. We quickly found each other because we were the two oldest students in the class. I was nearing thirty and he was nearing forty, and the rest of the class appeared to be in their early teens.

Shoichi was from Japan, but had spent a great deal of time in the U.S. over the past ten years. He was a mysterious sort of guy that had more life experiences than you might ever be willing to hear. He was an Olympic caliber athlete and was even scheduled to play for his national soccer team until an injury sidelined him. He was an expert martial artist, and won the state over-35 championship in tennis in California one year. He was an accomplished golfer as well.

Prior to going back to school, he had been one of the youngest vice presidents for Toyota Motor Company. He was also one of the youngest persons to ever take retirement in the company. His explanation, "Working eighteen hours a day, seven days a week is crazy." So he left the company at a very young age, moved to California and played golf and tennis every day. After a couple of years sating himself in sun and fun, he decided it was time to do something productive. He had a strong feeling that the elderly were a forgotten group in Japanese society, so he entered a master's program in gerontology at a university in Minnesota. While he was studying there, he met up with the department head at Maryland, and he made his way east to do his Ph.D. work.

The one thing that was hard to explain to people was how he made his expenses and paid tuition. One of those ways was through television. His work with Toyota was in public relations and he had a host of friends and colleagues working in radio, television and print media. The 1980's were a boom time for the Japanese economy, and the Japanese took every advantage they could to get their people to the U.S. Camera crews and directors were frequently doing projects in the U.S. and needed the services of folks like Shoichi to get them around, take care of details, and provide translation. Whenever a school break came around, Shoichi went to work, and he would often make enough money to keep himself in school for another semester.

Shoichi and I spent a great deal of time together not only in the books, but on the golf course. The University of Maryland's golf course had student memberships that cost a grand total of $50 dollars a year--unlimited play as long as you walked. After we had been studying together for a little over a year Shoichi asked me a strange question. "Do you like baseball?"

"Do I like baseball? I love baseball. Played it for years."

"What do you know about baseball?"

"About everything a guy needs to know."

"How about professional baseball?"

"I know more than average."

"I need your help."

I wasn't sure what that meant, but we were great friends and I would do anything I could to help him. Then he went into details. He told me that he took on too much work for the next spring break and thought that I would be able to handle one of his jobs. "I want you to go to Florida for Spring Training and talk to some baseball players."

"Are you kidding?"

"No, I need you to help me."

"Don't you have to have some kind of training to do that kind of thing."

"I never had any training."

"Don't I need some credentials or something?"

"We can take care of that."

He had been working part-time for Japan Broadcasting Corporation (N.H.K.) for about eight years, and he had been given letterhead to handle these very situations. "We'll write letters to the folks that need credentials and we'll tell them who you are."

"I'm a Ph.D. student at the University of Maryland."

"To them you will be a producer for N.H.K."

"You're sure I don't need a degree or something?"

His next words were prophetic, and may sum up all there is to know about the media, "It's television. Any fool can do television. You'll be fine."

We began pulling the story together in January of 1987. N.H.K. was doing a special about American baseball players that had played in Japan and then returned to the U.S. That year they were focusing on Bob Horner, who played all of one season in Japan and came home as quickly as he could-never to return. Horner had been a standout third baseman for the Atlanta Braves and was on a College World Series championship team from Arizona. His time in Japan was not a happy time and we were warned that he would not want to speak to us. Shoichi said, "All the more reason for you to go and not some Japanese guy."

Also featured in the story was Bill Madlock who was closing out a great career in Japan that season after playing for the Pittsburgh Pirates during their "We Are a Family" dynasty. Part of my time in Florida was to be spent talking with guys who played with the "Mad Dog" in the U.S. One other featured player was Davey Johnson who was then managing the Mets. Talking with professional baseball players is a dream come true for a red-blooded American nurtured on baseball. I was about to come face to face with that dream as soon as spring break began that March.

We had written letters to the St Louis Cardinals, the New York Mets, and the Atlanta Braves. I was guaranteed press passes when I got to Florida from all three of those clubs. I had a tentative interview with Bob Horner in St. Petersburg for a Monday around 12 noon when the team was taking batting practice.

I arrived on Sunday, went by the public relations office and got my passes and media kit. I was informed that the players union had a meeting scheduled for Monday at 11:00 a.m. It was possible that I couldn't get the interview that day. I had to make some snappy decisions. My camera crew was costing me $900 dollars per day, and if I couldn't get the interview, I would be spending a load of money that wasn't mine.

I called my cameraman in Miami, and asked him what he thought about postponing on Monday, and of course he told me that it was a silly idea (after all, that meant $900 dollars out of his pocket). He said it would be best to get the footage come hook or crook. So it was settled, I would see them around 11 a.m. in St. Pete, and we would talk to Bob Horner somehow.

I was at the stadium by 10 a.m. and there were dozens of reporters and camera crews hanging around, waiting for batting practice to start. The only one I recognized was Bob Costas from NBC, and he was working his throng of admirers. I watched him at work for about 30 minutes, and he had the best grasp of 1960's TV of anyone I have ever met. He could quote entire portions of "I Love Lucy" and "The Flintstones". He had the media in stitches as he signed autographs for the people gathered to see Spring Training baseball.

About the time my camera crew arrived, the PR guy came out and announced that the union meeting was going longer than expected, and that batting practice was scheduled in about 30 minutes. This meant less time with the players. I started to worry a bit, and then I began to question--"Who is Bob Costas here to interview?" The sound and light guy knew one of the NBC guys, so he went and asked. Costas was there to interview Bob Horner. I asked a few of the guys from local stations and newspapers who they were there to interview; most of them wanted Bob Horner.

The PR guy came out about 12 noon and said batting practice would not happen, but we would have about 30 minutes to do our interviews before game time. During this whole time, Bob Costas was walking in an out of the clubhouse as if he owned the place, and for all we knew he did. I looked at the clock, and it was obvious that game time was getting closer, and the likelihood of getting five minutes with Bob Horner was looking slim, so I began to organize the small market guys. They all knew I had to get my story for N.H.K. because I was out on a plane in the afternoon. I knew they all wanted a crack at him, so I said, "Let's get a group interview and he will be more likely to talk with us."

A reporter from Indiana agreed, and pretty soon I had ten cameras and light crews in a semi-circle in front of the dugout. As soon as Bob Horner poked his head out of the clubhouse, I invited him to our circle to save some time. He was happy to oblige. His voice became sarcastic when he heard I was from Japan Broadcasting Corporation, but he realized that all of the other guys would have him on film, so he kept it nice. (On the same day, there was a scathing article in the Tampa Tribune about how much Horner hated Japan, and how he regretted spending a year there.) The only question that I asked that got him riled was when I asked him about his "career in Japan." He grunted back, "I would hardly call a year a career." I asked him what he thought of that year, and he coolly replied, "A learning experience."

I turned over the questions to the other reporters and began to get some environment shots and began to enjoy my work in television. I looked over at Bob Costas and he was alone with a chair that was waiting for Bob Horner. It took about 20 minutes for Horner to leave the circle of reporters and make his way to Costas. By that time, the public address system was pumping upbeat music directly at the two interviewing. They got all of five minutes in before the call to clear the field of reporters went out. Costas was visibly angry, and even slapped himself with his notebook.

The NBC sound tech got word to my crew that Costas was not happy with me, and said I cost him the NBC interview. They mentioned that I better not be in Winterhaven tomorrow. No problem, I would be in Port St. Lucie.

My very first gig in television made me infamous. My camera crew loved me, and thought it was fascinating that a guy with a Master's of Divinity and nearly a Ph.D. in Recreation was spending his spring break in trouble with Bob Costas. I would soon discover that the next issue of Sports Illustrated featured Bob Horner, and included a picture of me leading my ring of reporters in St. Petersburg. All of this proving that "any fool can do television."

. . .

I flew that afternoon to West Palm Beach, and then drove up the coast to Port St. Lucie, where the New York Mets still have their spring home. I was to interview Davey Johnson, the manager of the Mets. Johnson had some good years in Japan and was at one time one of the most loved American players to play in Japan.

Before I left for Florida, Shoichi had given me $5,000 dollars in cash. By the time I had stopped in Port St. Lucie, I had already dropped $2,000 on a film crew plus their expenses. I realized when I pulled into the Holiday Inn and registered for my room that I was living a different lifestyle than I ever imagined. I had never made a salary of more than $1,500 per month, and here I had already blown $2,000 in a couple of days. I began to wonder, "How could I have a future in a business that spent so much money? How could I have a future carrying that much cash around?"

I was scheduled to be at the ballpark at 11:00 AM. It was not a game day, so I would have better access to Johnson. The film crew met me there after driving up from Miami. We checked in with the public relations office, and went out to the field. I saw Davey Johnson and my PR contact in heated conversation near the pitcher's mound. I couldn't help but think it had something to do with us.

A few moments later the PR guy came and told us that Johnson felt he had been deceived and that we were not with N.H.K. I asked what made him think that. "You didn't bring gifts."

The long-held Japanese custom of gift giving was something that Johnson loved while he played in that country. He was a national hero, and national heroes got Cuban cigars, expensive whiskeys and liquor, and sometimes jewelry before interviews. The three wise guys that showed up at the ballpark that day came bearing a camera, a microphone, and a letter saying that we were there to interview Davey Johnson.

"Is he going to do the interview or not?" I asked the PR guy.

"I am embarrassed to say, but he is not planning to do one with you."

"So I have just laid out good money on a camera crew, and we confirmed with you last week that we had the interview, and now your manager won't talk with us because we didn't bring him gifts?"

"That's what it looks like."

"You realize that I will have to do that story don't you? TV folks don't mind telling negative stories, especially since it is already paid for."

"Let me get back with you in a second."

The PR guy went back to the mound and obviously shared the news with Johnson. Johnson was livid.

But he came over to the third base side and did an interview with us. He was very professional, very courteous, answered all of our questions politely, and sent thanks to the Japanese people for the years he spent there. When the camera stopped rolling, and I thanked him for his time he yelled at me, "Get the hell out of here. I don't want to see you again." He can be assured that this will not happen.

...

The next day was spent in West Palm Beach at the Braves camp. I had interviews scheduled with Chuck Tanner, the former manager of the Pittsburgh Pirates, and Willie Stargell who was then an assistant with the Braves. Tanner managed Stargell and Bill Madlock in Pittsburgh during the peak of the "We Are a Family" years. Madlock was playing in Japan that season, and the Japanese wanted quotes from friends and what they thought of him playing overseas.

I arrived at the ballpark a little early and they sent me out to the field to wait on my interviewees. I found Ozzie Virgil, who was the starting catcher for the Braves, flying a remote control airplane. I got the camera crew to film this unexpected scene as I talked with Ozzie. He asked what I was doing there, and when he found out I was with N.H.K. he asked, "You think they might help me get a gig with the remote control airplane folks in Japan?" I said that I doubted I could make that happen.

"Man, the Japanese have the best remote control stuff in the business. I would love to do a commercial for them."

About that time a gust of wind sent his plane out of control and he crashed it in the middle of the centerfield grass. All of this caught on tape. A couple of months later when I saw the final cut of the video, they actually used this footage to show the difference between American and Japanese players. The Japanese would never consider playing with toys before baseball practice. But they also admitted that American players have more fun.

Tanner gave the typical clichéd congratulatory stuff you might expect from a coach. Stargell was a different story. My first question was, "If you had something to say to Madlock about playing in Japan, what would you have to offer?" Stargell went into an expletive laced comment challenging Madlock's manhood, his mother and his patriotism. I asked Stargell if he knew he was on camera, and he replied, "Hell yes, keep it rolling." I learned later that Stargell and Madlock were very close friends and that talking trash was how they communicated. This was not apparent to the video editors so very little of that interview made it on the program.

...

My first two jobs in television were in sports: baseball and then golf. I consider sports to be the easy way to break into television because a more fun loving, laid back crowd, generally runs it. On the other hand, I didn't find it mentally challenging. The athletes that I kept running into didn't have much of a life off the field, and not many interests beyond their sport and what they watched on ESPN the night before.

After all of my coursework was done at the university, I went to work full-time with N.H.K., and for about seven months I stayed on the road, made good money and dealt with more interesting people.

On one occasion we were in Orlando and then Cape Canaveral to film a documentary on the aftermath of the Challenger Space Shuttle disaster in which a Japanese astronaut lost his life. I learned the power of connections during that trip. When we arrived at NASA with our letter to film, and they gave us our security clearances, their staff did not include in the list of available film sites the specific areas that the director wanted to shoot.

When this colonel in the Air Force came out and yelled at us that there was no way we were going into some of those restricted areas, I was fine with his answers and would have said no problem. Shoichi would not be deterred. He got on the phone with somebody in Japan, and within twenty minutes we had the okay to see almost anything we wanted. The young sergeant that was assigned to us for the day remarked to me, "You realize that you are the only outside film crew to ever be in the assembly building?"

"What do you mean? I have seen this on television before."

"Those were Air Force photographers and that was footage all pre-approved by the Pentagon. You are doing something brand new here."

To this day I don't know whom Shoichi called, but I am certain that I would not feel comfortable in their presence.

We celebrated that night at a famous restaurant in Orlando. One of the jobs of producing is to make sure food and accommodations are taken care of. Most of the crews that came from Japan had very specific recommendations from travel books or magazine articles. I can't remember the name of this restaurant, but I do know it had five stars beside it in the magazine article and was considered the most expensive restaurant in the city.

There were eight of us at dinner, and they gave us a private area that overlooked a fountain and light display. One of the things I had to learn in the business was that when a Japanese film crew went out drinking at the end of the day, they were serious about it.

Immediately after we arrived they ordered two rounds of drinks before the menu ever arrived. The menu was not very large, a few steaks, a few seafood dishes, and some ala Carte dishes, but it was the most expensive menu I had ever seen in my life. The baked potato was $20 dollars. A salad was $25. The wines ranged from $75 to $500 dollars a bottle. I picked up the bill at the end of the night, and I couldn't believe it--$2,300 dollars for eight people. I went into my brief case and kept pulling out cash. A very different world.

From Orlando, the crew was headed for New York to talk to a couple of scientists that were not at all pleased with NASA. We spent a couple of days before Christmas chasing down these guys and getting some interviews on film. We were supposed to break for Christmas and meet again in Boston after January 1st. On December 23rd we ate a big meal together at Wollensky's-- where the prices were "more normal" according to Shoichi. All extra items on the menu were $5 dollars- baked potato, vegetables, salads. All of the steaks were paid by the ounce, and generally ran about $70 dollars a person. I remember laying nearly a thousand dollars out that night for the group, and one of them remarked: "Not bad prices." It wasn't until I lived in Japan that I understood that they might think that way.

By the 24th, my brief case was out of cash. I had spent somewhere around $15,000 dollars in the past week, and I wasn't picking up all of the bills. I had tickets back to my home in Maryland for the holidays, and before I left Shoichi handed me $12,000 dollars to handle expenses in Boston after the New Year. It was one thing to be carrying all of that money for the group with the group. Now I was on my own on my way out of New York with a pile of cash. Let's just say that uncomfortable would not get to the bottom of my feelings.

I got a cab to LaGuardia on Christmas Eve, and my cabbie was in full Christmas spirit. He was weaving in an out of traffic like a wild man, and I knew that he was making people mad. At one stoplight a guy got out of his car and walked up to the cab with a gun in his hand and told the cabbie to "settle down or I will blow you away." I can't say that I know what the mafia looks like, but if I had to make a guess, he would have been it. The cabbie just brushed the comment away with a "Merry Christmas, man."

I lay down in the seat hoping that I would not be shot along with my cab driver. The money in my brief case was actually the least of my worries in route to the airport. Arriving alive was much more important.

When I arrived at the terminal, I witnessed a purse snatching, and no less than two people being hauled away by policeman. I thought what a postcard touch that would be to have a picture of a woman crying hysterically with two guys being shoved into a police car--Merry Christmas from New York.

After checking in for an 8:00 p.m. flight, I looked at the runway and there was nothing taking off or landing. "Too much fog," someone said. They made an announcement at 7:45 p.m. that if we wanted to try to get on the 9 p.m. flight out of Kennedy Airport, we could get on a bus and they would hold the flight. I knew I had to be home for the holidays. In fact, we were leaving out at 5:00 a.m. the next morning to see in-laws in Pennsylvania, so I got on the bus.

As you might expect, it was foggy at Kennedy and they were saying that it might be 10:00 a.m. before we could get out the next morning--Christmas Day. I had some decisions to make. Would I attempt to get home, or try and meet the family in Pennsylvania?

It was a holiday, so there were no rental cars to be found in all of New York. And there was one last train leaving New York for Washington at 11:30 p.m. I reserved a ticket and headed back to the city for Grand Central station. In the process, I had met two guys who spoke almost no English, but who were headed the same place I was. The guy from Russia spoke some German and the guy from China spoke a little English, and the three of us took off for the train together. We got to the station and had about an hour to kill, so we stepped over the drug dealers and winos that were lying all over the station. I recalled that I was carrying more cash than I ever cared to lose, and I was making it home for the holidays with Russian and a Chinese businessman in tow. A surreal picture if there ever were one.

After the train was delayed several times by fog, I finally arrived home about 5:30 a.m. on Christmas morning. We were to leave for Pennsylvania thirty minutes earlier. I asked Diane to call them and say we would be a couple hours late. I got a nap, and then we got in the car and headed to her sister's place.

We kept the cash in my briefcase locked in the trunk, and forever I can say that getting home for Christmas was never again that eventful.

Back to Church

When I left Dozier, Alabama in 1982, it appeared that I spent eight years doing just about everything I could do to avoid returning to the local church as pastor. I had been among other things a camp director, a college instructor, a television producer and a research assistant. I had traveled the country, spent lots of someone else's money, and about the time I turned thirty I needed to make some decisions about my future. What happened was that my future made some decisions for me.

Diane and I were living in Washington, DC, the second most expensive city in the country at that time. We were paying about $700 dollars a month rent for a crumbling third floor apartment in a decaying neighborhood. Contrast this with the payment we made for the only home we ever owned (ten years later, no less)--$415 dollars per month--and it seems outrageous. Between the two of us we were making about $30,000 steady dollars a year, but after rent, utilities, insurance, car payment and food, we were nearly broke every month.

I got news from the recreation department in the fall of 1989 that since my course work was done and my comprehensive exams were completed, I could continue teaching at the university, but not under a teaching assistantship which paid much better. I would have to let another student take my place and become those dirty words: "adjunct faculty." I did the math and figured that my salary would be cut in half and I would lose my benefits if I continued to teach. So I went looking for a real job. The television business was still viable, but not reliable money. I could not count on it for paying bills mainly just luxury stuff. So I was in a dilemma.

There were not any local jobs for an A.B.D. (all but dissertation), and Washington was well known for its tight job market, so I started looking outside of my field. What I ended up with was a job in construction. There was an independent contractor building custom homes just a five-minute walk from where I lived. The pay was not great, but I actually made more than I did teaching, and almost as much as Diane did in her professional job downtown. Most appealing was when I left the job site I never had a paper to grade, or another book to read. I had a 5-minute commute by foot, and I became strong and learned some skills I had never used before.

My boss was a patient guy, and put up with my lack of carpentry skills because I was dependable. His very words to me when I left the job in December were: "You are not very skilled, but damnit you were here every day on time, and you gave me a full day's work and that's more than I can say for the rest of the crew."

We both knew the truth because from August to December, the first thing I did at the job site nearly every Monday morning was go by one of the crew's house and make sure he was up. While I was there, I usually called the other experienced guy on the crew to make sure he was alive and was headed to work. I had usually put in two hours for the boss before the whole crew arrived on Monday. On Fridays, around quitting time, it was usually the boss and me left to put up the tools and equipment for the weekend because the rest of the crew found excuses to leave early all through the day. I will never forget one Friday being asked to haul a truckload of construction waste to the landfill. Jimmy had gotten off early for a doctor's appointment and Ben said he had to meet his girlfriend early to go to a funeral. On my way to the landfill, I passed a small tavern, and there were the two of them drinking beer on a Friday afternoon. The boss knew what was going on, but he reasoned that they put in a solid thirty hours a week, and that was worth more to him than hiring another carpenter.

Around November, Diane got word that the funding for her organization had been suspended for the next year, and so she was given her three months' notice. I was in a job that I could leave at the drop of a hat, and she was in a job that had already dropped the hat. We figured we could survive a couple of months in Washington without jobs, so we had to look for alternatives.

We spent Thanksgiving at her folk's retirement home in the mountains of North Carolina. It was a place we loved, and a house we helped build. We got this hair-brained idea that maybe we could move to Lake Junaluska. Her folks were understanding and basically appreciated having someone to look after the house for the eleven months that nobody was there. We made the decision that we would look for jobs, and would come if either one of us found a job. Diane drew that straw and became the director of a crisis center. It was then up to me to find a job within that community to help pay the bills.

Haywood County was known more for its poor literacy rate than it was for its economic opportunities. So it was readily apparent that I was over-qualified for most of the jobs in the area. No one wanted to hire a guy with a master's degree and especially someone who had nearly completed a Ph.D. The couple of jobs that did give me a look warned me that I had good qualifications, but they were more likely to hire someone who was a permanent resident because they were more likely to stay put for a long period of time. When I explained that I had every intention of staying around, they would return to the fact that I was over-qualified and that I would be bored with what they could give me to do and with the money they were willing to pay. I can't fault them for their honesty.

After being in town a couple of months, and becoming known as a full-time volunteer for various groups, someone came and offered me a job. The pastor of the church that we had been attending was very understanding and knew I had no intentions of going into the ministry for a living, but that they could use me as a part-time youth director while I explored other options. What ended up happening was that I never got around to exploring other options, I enjoyed my work too much.

I went from part-time to full-time over the next half year, and got back to the roots of my first work out of high school. It was not long before I had developed the job from youth director into associate pastor, and went from working primarily with youth and children to the entire congregation. I had made a move back to the very kind of job I had been trying to avoid for the eight previous years. You might say that God works in strange and mysterious ways.

I stayed at that church as an assistant in Lake Junaluska for three and a half years before moving to a church of my own in Mayodan, North Carolina. Since then I have served the past six years in three different settings. I still wonder what I will do when I grow up, and I keep wondering when that will be.

Nearly every week I am called on to do the very thing I enjoy doing the most, and that is to tell stories in front of people (That is in one sense what preacher's do.). And almost every week I am called on to teach, something that I am gifted to do. The process of teaching and telling stories means that I spend a great deal of time reading and studying as well as writing, things that bring great pleasure to my life. All of these things that are satisfying to me are part of a larger purpose, and bring meaning to my life and others.

The past twelve years of serving in the church have brought me more stories than I will ever have time to tell or write down, but I share a couple of them as examples of what my life back in the church has been like...

Traveling with youth in a church van

As a youth director in the mountains of North Carolina, a prerequisite is a driver's license. There's not going to be much ministry done relying on public transportation, since there is none. Non-motorized means of travel are just impractical, and if you can drive, you will become a taxi or bus service. That's one of the hazards of the job.

In my years as a youth director, I traveled thousands of miles with youth in the church van. Almost guaranteed every year were trips from Lake Junaluska to Durham, Charlotte, Atlanta, and to Ash County. Then there were occasional trips like the one to Louisville, Kentucky or the one to Charleston, South Carolina. Not to mention regular trips to the mountain metropolis of Asheville that was only twenty-five miles away.

I discovered that traveling with youth is one of the best ways to get to know them. The true character of a person comes out when you get them away from home and familiar surroundings. And there is nothing that tests character like eight hours with a van full of teenagers.

The trip to Durham every year was to see Duke football. The university would sell thousands of discount tickets to Methodist churches across the state in hopes of filling up the stadium once each season. They would add a youth speaker and some extra fun stuff to the schedule and call it "Youth Day."

The festivities would always begin around 10 a.m., and the game at 12 noon. Those of us in the mountains always had a four to five hour drive, meaning that in order to get there for the fun stuff, we would have to leave between five and six in the morning. We always compromised, and said it was more important to leave later in the morning, and catch some of the fun, and all of the game. So for three years in a row, I would load up youth at 6:30 a.m. on a crisp fall Saturday morning and head east to Durham.

Nearly every year, I had Donnie as my co-pilot because nobody else wanted to sit next to him. Donnie was a smart kid with terrible social skills. He knew the ins and outs of many subjects and was a whiz with math, but "does not play well with others" was certainly the regular note teachers sent home to his parents. The other youth treated him poorly, and it didn't seem to matter to Donnie, he never changed his tone or attitude, and remained obnoxious the entire time I was at the church. He went off to college and blossomed they say. He was like a fruit tree that takes years to produce fruit.

So all the way to Durham, Donnie was reading the signs, asking me questions, and basically staying out of the others' hair. Because I was the driver, I got to make rules about the radio. It was a four-hour drive, so we had to listen to four different kinds of music on the way there and on the way back. If they didn't like what was on the radio, they didn't have to listen.

So we would listen to a local pop station out of Asheville for the first hour, then change to a country station out of Charlotte for the second hour, then change to a Contemporary Christian station out of Greensboro for hour three, and then the final leg was always an oldies station. The return trip was usually the reverse of the trip down the mountain.

Nearly every trip, I would have a similar crowd riding with me. Usually my pop music aficionados sat in the back, with the country music fans in front of them, and the ones who liked contemporary Christian and oldies in the seat right behind me. Donnie was always in the seat to my right, and he disliked all the music. He would listen to Weird Al Yankovich on his Walkman for eight hours at the time.

The two seats in the back of the van would spend most of the trip talking about the opposite sex, and making fun of each other. The kids right behind me would talk about sensitive things like world peace and the homeless. And Donnie would always interrupt all of the conversations with something crude like, "You know, I am about to fart. I suggest you hold your breath."

The other adults that would ride with me never understood how I could stand these trips. "How do you tune out all of this juvenile talk and behavior?" I guess because I never tuned it out. I was always trying to enter their world, and trying to get a handle on what made them tick. And the van was one of the best places to discover who they were.

If you were real observant, you could see the changes that took place in them as they left Haywood County and headed down the mountain. Though the interstate is pretty uniform for much of the trip, somehow when we got to the bigger cities of Winston-Salem and Greensboro, they began to get quiet. There's something about seeing a building over three stories tall that changes your perspective. Seeing real traffic is an avenue to personal growth. The back rows would begin talking about where they wanted to go to college and what they wanted to do when they grew up. The row behind me would talk about what it would be like to be the governor or congressman. Donnie would always interrupt with a question like: "How long do you think it would take an ambulance to get here if the van blew up?"

One of the truths that I have discovered about youth ministry is that the destination is usually less memorable than the travel to and from. Every year the Duke football game and the Youth Day events were a bust. We actually saw more exciting football on Friday nights in Haywood County than we ever saw in Durham.

But we would always tack on a visit to Duke Chapel and the university campus and I would watch their jaws drop. If the organ was playing in the chapel at the time, you could see this sense of awe overcome them. I am convinced that was what the organ was invented for, to give you a taste of the awesomeness of God. Gothic architecture with its massive stone buildings has a way of altering the perceptions of mountain youth. It was always the highlight of the day for me to hear them asking each other, "Do you think I will ever make the grades to get into a place like this?"

We would get back on the road to the mountains late in the afternoon, anticipating that we would get back home by ten o'clock.

We would turn on the oldies station, and I would discover that even though I was fifteen to twenty years older than most of these kids, we held something in common--an appreciation for the music of the 1960's. They knew the Beatles, Elvis, and the Rolling Stones. We would be headed up the road singing Motown and Bob Dylan together. It was the one area where our generations shared a common thread and it always surprised me.

When we turned on the contemporary Christian station, they would sit back and get reflective. They would talk about meaningful things like marriage and family (of course, that was the back two rows). The row right behind me would talk about becoming missionaries, or social workers. Donnie would often ask: "Do you think I will be a different guy when I get to college?"

When the country station was locked in, the whole van would sing country music together. As bad as they hated to admit it, they were all "country, when country wasn't cool." Even the kids that were too cool for country music knew all the words, and nobody in the van called them on it. Even Donnie knew country music, and for an hour we would have a great time together singing and laughing.

The last hour, was always my favorite. The Asheville station would be pumping out top-forty music, and three-quarters of the van would be asleep. Then I could talk quietly with my serious kids in the seat behind me, and Donnie would listen attentively.

The last bit of road between Asheville and Lake Junaluska was always the quietest. Those that weren't asleep were pondering the day's events. It was during that time that I would look back on how that group of teenagers amused me so. Even ten years later, when I get behind the wheel of a van, I still think back to those days on the road with my youth.

The baby is born

When I was thirty-three, and Diane was thirty-two, we had our first and only child. His story has influenced all others since then. Like most people's children, he is a special child. He began his life in a special way as the child not only of two parents, but also of an entire church community.

To give you an idea of how his life began, we can trace back to a year before. At that time, Diane and I were serving in two different churches and living in two different houses on opposite sides of a mountain in Western North Carolina. It was around my thirty-second birthday that we decided that if we were going to plunge into real adulthood, we might want to consider living in the same home and raising children of our own, instead of our churches' children.

The only way for us to do that was to change positions and make a drastic move. So we began the process of looking at the future and putting our name into the pot of those United Methodist preachers scheduled to move the next summer.

In December we made the decision to move, in January we decided we would begin actually trying to have children, and in February we took a vacation to Mexico since we figured it would be awhile before we would get another.

In March, the mountains of North Carolina were blanketed with the highest snowfall in recent history. It just so happens we were both at the same house (and snowed in with the in-laws no less) when 24 inches of snow fell and shut everything down for almost a week. In April, we discovered that Diane was expecting and the baby was due in December (Also note that the largest number of babies born in Western North Carolina in history all appeared around nine months after the great snowstorm.) In May we found out where we were moving, and in June we moved. An eventful six months if ever there was.

We moved to the town of Mayodan, North Carolina that was a small mill town wedged into the foothills of the Appalachian range. We were only about a ten-minute drive to Virginia. Neither of us had ever heard of the town until we had been assigned there. It became four of the most pleasant years that we have ever spent anywhere.

We arrived in June, and by that time Diane was beginning to show that she was expecting. It had been awhile since the church had a new baby in its parsonage, so they were extra gracious to us. They knew that she wasn't due until December, but you would have thought the fuss they made over her that it was due in a few weeks.

We endured a warm summer and were almost startled by the fall that arrives with gusto in the mountain country. The leaves changing color and crisp air were beautiful that year. We spent September and October on Thursday nights at the Women's Hospital in Greensboro going through birthing classes. We were learning all about natural childbirth and were anticipating that day in December when the baby would arrive.

As the fall crept along, the baby crept lower and lower on Diane's torso. There was no doubt that the baby was going to be a big one, because Diane had gotten very large. Every check-up revealed new information. We decided early on that we wanted to know its gender, and when we saw the first sonogram it was quite evident that we were going to have a little boy since the doctor counted ten fingers, ten toes and another finger toward the middle of the body.

In the seventh month, the doctor showed us sonograms of how the baby was wedged in her uterus and that it was highly possible that he would not travel down the birth canal correctly. This left open the option for a Cesarean section, but they would make that decision later.

When the eighth month came around, appointments began to be every week. They poked and prodded and checked everything each week. The doctors were still concerned about the blood pressure, and had made a definite decision to do the C-section, now the only decision was when.

The due date was December 15th, but based on measurements and calculations, they figured the baby would be over 10 pounds by then. Diane was scheduled for an appointment on the Monday before Thanksgiving. It was at this meeting that the doctors would determine a delivery date and we could schedule the hospital.

During the appointment, Diane had a headache, her blood pressure was a little higher than normal, and another test showed some further signs of stress. The doctor told us to make an appointment for anytime the next week, and urged Diane to relax and rest for the next 5-7 days. Diane asked the doctor if it would be okay for her to travel a couple of hours to her parent's house for Thanksgiving. He replied immediately, "I recommend that you don't."

We walked out of the doctor's office and I asked her when she wanted to schedule the hospital. She said that she would think about it. On the drive home she thought how silly it was that she was not able to travel to her folks for Thanksgiving. "If I can't go anywhere for Thanksgiving I might as well have the baby."

I tried to reason with her, that maybe Thanksgiving was not the best time to have a baby since the hospital staff will be on a holiday schedule, and the doctors would probably be out of town. "Not if we have the baby before they leave," was her retort.

On Tuesday she woke up with a pounding headache, and she figured her blood pressure was very high. "I think I need to have the baby this week," was what she told me at breakfast. "That's between you and the doctors, I am staying out of this."

Tuesday morning she got on the phone and told the doctors of her situation (not mentioning anything about being mad about not being able to travel on Thanksgiving) and they suggested that she come in on Wednesday morning. If everything tested out, they would schedule her for a C-section late on Wednesday afternoon before the holidays. She called me while I was at the office and said that I'd better make arrangements for the Community Thanksgiving Service that was scheduled for our church on Wednesday night, "We are going to have a baby tomorrow."

I asked, "Is that what the doctor said?"

"Not exactly. But if everything tests out correctly, we could have the baby Wednesday evening."

I had already learned after nine years of marriage not to question any further. If Diane planned to have the baby on Wednesday, she would have the baby. Her determination is that strong. By Wednesday morning, she was exhibiting every symptom that could possibly speed up the delivery of the baby. Headache, nausea, sweating all accompanied our visit. The doctor took a quick urine test and a blood pressure check, and said that the only thing that would stop him from doing the procedure today was the test on the baby's lungs. It involved sticking a huge needle into Diane's stomach and into the birth fluids. The actual needle part was about thirty minutes; the results would come three hours later.

"You guys go home, and we'll call you if you need to come back."

"But it's a forty-five minute drive home, can we wait here in Greensboro."

"As long as Diane relaxes."

"Good, I can go get some lunch," she said.

"No lunch. No food until after the procedure, if we do it."

"I can have food can't I doctor?" I asked jokingly.

"By all means, and I suggest you have a beer or something stronger. You need to relax too."

So we weighed our options. There weren't many places to just sit and relax in Greensboro. The mall was out of the question because that meant walking. We could go to the library, but it was pain to drive and park. Then Diane suggested we go to a movie, "There must be one showing in the middle of the day somewhere."

She was right. Just a few minutes from the doctor's office was a small theater, and one of the movies showing was one that we wanted to see. "Mrs. Doubtfire" had been playing for several weeks, and we had never seen it, so we got two tickets to the 1:30 p.m. show. The doctor said to call back to the office about 2:30 p.m. for the results.

We watched the first hour of the movie, and Diane called in, using the phone next to the popcorn machine. "Congratulations," the receptionist said, "the results came in and you can have the baby today. Can you be at the hospital at 4:00 p.m.?"

"No problem," Diane told her, "the movie will be over at 3:30."

She came back and told me in the middle of the movie, the part where Robin Williams has infiltrated his ex's home and is the nanny for his own children. She then went back to the lobby to call her parents and family. "Let me know what I missed," she said.

So I watched the rest of the movie, but didn't remember much of it because my mind was on other things. When she came back to her seat, I went out and called the folks that I had left in charge of the Community Thanksgiving Service. I wanted to confirm that I would not be at the church that night.

I returned to my seat and watched the last part of the movie. It was a cleverly done role by Robin Williams that was both humorous and touching, and a movie about parenthood. How fitting for our last afternoon as DINKS (Double Income No Kids).

We showed up at the hospital about 4:00 p.m. and began processing the paperwork (the paper work would not be finished for about 18 months, but that is another story altogether). At 4:30 p.m. we were in a pre-op room and Diane was fitted with IV's and given painkiller. At 5:00 p.m. we went into the operating room. I got to view the whole thing, and it is not a pretty site to see your wife's inner organs plopped out on her stomach.

At 5:17 p.m. the doctors pulled out a greasy baby boy with fine, curly blond hair. He was named Jeremiah after the prophet who was known by God in the womb. The doctors left the operating room to spend Thanksgiving with their families. Our little family spent Thanksgiving in the hospital. It was a Thanksgiving that we will remember always.

Then began one of the most trying, yet important jobs I will ever have—the job of parenting.

www.ingramcontent.com/pod-product-compliance
Lightning Source LLC
Chambersburg PA
CBHW030356290526
45785CB00004B/1774